AF528547

DEVELOPMENT
EXPERIENCES, INSIGHTS AND INTROSPECTION

DEVELOPMENT
EXPERIENCES, INSIGHTS AND INTROSPECTION

VIPIN SHARMA

Orient BlackSwan

All rights reserved. No part of this book may be modified, reproduced or utilised in any form, or by any means, electronic or mechanical, including photocopying, recording or by any information storage and retrieval system, in any form of binding or cover other than in which it is published, without permission in writing from the publisher.

DEVELOPMENT: EXPERIENCES, INSIGHTS AND INTROSPECTION

ORIENT BLACKSWAN PRIVATE LIMITED

Registered Office
3-6-752 Himayatnagar, Hyderabad 500 029, Telangana, India
e-mail: centraloffice@orientblackswan.com

Other Offices
Bengaluru, Chennai, Guwahati, Hyderabad, Kolkata, Mumbai, New Delhi, Noida, Patna, Visakhapatnam

© Vipin Sharma 2021
First published by Orient Blackswan Private Limited 2021
First reprint 2022
Second reprint 2022
Third reprint 2022

P-ISBN: 978-93-5442-090-0
E-ISBN: 978-93-5442-098-6

033918

Typeset in
Sabon LT Std 11.5/14.5
by Manmohan Kumar, Delhi

Printed in India at
Thomson Press, New Delhi 110 020

Published by
Orient Blackswan Private Limited
3-6-752 Himayatnagar, Hyderabad 500 029, Telangana, India
e-mail: info@orientblackswan.com

This book is purely a personal academic endeavour, and meant for academic purpose only. The views and opinions expressed in this book are the author's own. These views and opinions do not necessarily represent official policy or position of the Government of India, Government of Maharashtra, University of Sussex and the Institute of Development Studies. The facts and figures are as reported by the author, which have been verified to the extent possible, and the publishers are not in any way liable for the same. The development themes covered in this book being dynamic in nature, need to be perused in the time context of original writings, as the present circumstances may have changed. Readers' discretion is advised in all such situations. All sources and references used in this book are in public domain and appear in the consolidated bibliography at the end of the book. The figures and tables used in this book have been either used with permission, or duly credited and linked back to their original sources, or believed to be a fair use of such adapted and adopted material. The author is the sole contributor of this volume and asserts the moral right to be identified as the author of this book. The copyright in this book is the sole and absolute property of the author during the legal term of copyright.

CONTENTS

TABLES AND FIGURES

Tables

Figures

ABBREVIATIONS

BLTF	Bodo Liberation Tigers Force
BOP	Balance of Payments
BRI	Belt and Road Initiative
BRICS	Brazil, Russia, India, China, South Africa
CAA	Civil Aviation Authority
CGST	Central GST
CIS	Commonwealth of Independent States
CSIS	Center for Strategic and International Studies
DAC	Development Assistance Committee
DFID	Department for International Development
DGS&D	Directorate General of Supplies and Disposals
DPA	Development Partner Administration
EU	European Union
FC	Finance Commission
FDI	Foreign Direct Investment
G8	Group of 8
G20	Group of 20
G77	Group of 77
GDP	Gross Domestic Product
GeM	Government e-Marketplace
GeMSPV	GeM Special Purpose Vehicle
GST	Goods and Services Tax
GSTC	GST Council
GSTN	GST Network
HDI	Human Development Index
HDR	Human Development Report

HIPCs	Highly Indebted Poor Countries
HYVP	High Yielding Varieties Programme
IADP	Intensive Agricultural District Programme
IAEA	International Atomic Energy Agency
IAS	Indian Administrative Service
IBSA	India, Brazil, South Africa
ICCR	Indian Council for Cultural Relations
IDI	India Development Initiative
IDS	Institute of Development Studies
IEG	Institute of Economic Growth
IFAD	International Fund for Agricultural Development
IGST	Integrated GST
IHDI	Inequality-adjusted Human Development Index
IMF	International Monetary Fund
IMTRAT	Indian Military Training Team
INSTC	International North-South Transport Corridor
IOR	Indian Ocean Region
IRDP	Integrated Rural Development Programme
IT	Information Technology
ITC	Input Tax Credit
ITEC	Indian Technical and Economic Cooperation
KLO	Kamtapur Liberation Organisation
KYC	Know your Customer
LOC	Line of Credit
MCA	Ministry of Corporate Affairs
MDGs	Millennium Development Goals
MEA	Ministry of External Affairs
MGNREGA	Mahatma Gandhi National Rural Employment Guarantee Act

MGNREGS	Mahatma Gandhi National Rural Employment Guarantee Scheme
MMT	Million Metric Ton
MSEs	Micro and Small Enterprises
MSMEs	Micro, Small and Medium Enterprises
MSP	Minimum Support Price
MT	Metric Ton
MW	Mega Watt
NAM	Non-Aligned Movement
NDA	National Democratic Alliance
NDFB	National Democratic Front of Bodoland
NPAs	Non-Performing Assets
NRBAs	Non-Resident Baht Accounts
NREGA	National Rural Employment Guarantee Act
NREP	National Rural Employment Programme
ODA	Overseas Development Assistance
OECD	Organisation of Economic Cooperation and Development
OIC	Organisation of Islamic Conference
PAN	Permanent Account Number
PAPs	Poverty Alleviation Programmes
PFM	Public Financial Management
PPP	Purchasing Power Parity
PTA	Preferential Trade Agreement
RLEGS	Rural Landless Employment Guarantee Scheme
SAARC	South Asian Association for Regional Cooperation
SAC	South Asia Corridor
SBI	State Bank of India
SCAAP	Special Commonwealth African Assistance Program

SGST	State GST
SLOCs	Sea Lines of Communication
SSC	South-South Cooperation
TEC	Technical and Economic Cooperation
UAE	United Arab Emirates
UK	United Kingdom
ULFA	United Liberation Front of Assam
UN	United Nations
UNDP	United Nations Development Programme
UNSC	United Nations Security Council
USA	United States of America
USSR	Union of Soviet Socialist Republics
VAT	Value-Added Tax
WB	World Bank
WDR	World Development Report
WTO	World Trade Organization

FOREWORD

Development – disruptions, definitions and debate

We live in an era of major global disruptions and challenges, from pandemics such as Covid-19, to those related to climate and environmental change, health, technology, conflict, migration, rapid urbanisation and democratic disorder. Development Studies is critical to understanding and addressing such challenges, generating and mobilising research that crosses boundaries – disciplinary, sectoral, and national. It tackles global issues while remaining grounded in the day-to-day realities of people's lives. It seeks not only to understand the world, but also to change it for the better. Such values are central to our research, teaching and learning at the Institute of Development Studies (IDS), where the reflections and insights conveyed in this book, with the focus on India, were formed.

If this captures something of what development studies is about, then what is 'development'? Meanings are diverse, contested and changing. For some, development is inextricably entangled with ideas of modernisation, linear progress and the transfer of resources and knowledge from 'developed' to 'developing' nations. Development thus means the institutions, discourses and practices established in the post-Second World War period and applied to newly independent countries through international agencies such as the World Bank, reproduced and adapted to the present through a growing 'aid industry' involving multiple donor agencies, consultants, governmental and non-governmental organisations.

However, this view of development as aid, planning and projects is open to critique, both for presuming that some should define and steer 'progress' for others, and for its narrow view of change. Another broad meaning of development is economic, social, political and technological change that leads to better lives. This opens up appreciation of a far wider range of actors and influences, including states, businesses, social movements, media and more. It allows us to pluralise 'development', appreciating diverse views and experiences of change, and of 'good' and 'better'. As this book discusses, economic growth, employment levels, effective democracies, human development and poverty reduction, all offer different perspectives on what the outcomes of development might be, and how they should be measured. These have been part of India's development debate, often in contested ways. Of growing importance are perspectives, that define 'good change' in terms of reduced inequalities of multiple kinds, environmental sustainability, and citizen empowerment – seeking inclusive politics that support people's power to choose and achieve social justice.

India provides a remarkable lens for exploring and reflecting on development – its past, present and future. The country's size, history, vigorous and sophisticated scholarship, active civil society, and growing presence on the world stage heighten the significance of debates about the processes and outcomes of development domestically, as well as what lessons India might offer to the world. As this book documents, India now counts itself amongst development donors, in a global context in which the old categories of 'developed' and 'developing' countries, 'North' and 'South', are increasingly challenged by evidence of poverty, inequality, health and environmental problems in countries of Europe and North America, as well as Asia, Africa and Latin America. Development is now recognised as relevant for everyone everywhere, in Brighton, as much as in Bengaluru, Bamako or Bogota – as emphasised in the 'universal' framing of the United Nations Agenda 2030 (Sustainable Development Goals), calling for transformations towards more sustainable and prosperous futures for people and planet.

The experiences and insights in this book cover many themes, while focusing especially on economic aspects of development. It relates a largely positive narrative of India's development, one that reflects the experiences and position of its author as an academic, with a background in the Indian Administrative Service. The picture, as all development pictures, is partial, and would likely be contested by others – academics more concerned with social justice, inequality, gender or environment perhaps, or those rooted in India's rich social movements and civil society. Ongoing and vigorous debate, involving critique and contestation over development knowledge, meanings and practices is vital; it is central to the work ethos at the IDS, and to the wider field of development studies. I welcome this book as one set of experiences, insights and introspection about Indian development, put together with clarity and honesty.

With new topics and manifestations constantly emerging, development studies is an endlessly lively and wide-ranging field. Yet some key features hold it together. One is interdisciplinarity: scholars include anthropologists, economists, sociologists, political scientists, geographers and other social scientists; increasingly working also with those from the arts, humanities and natural sciences. A second is an engaged perspective, sometimes referred to as transdisciplinarity, in which research and knowledge are co-constructed with non-academic actors such as policymakers, practitioners, social movements, businesses or community organisations; thereby improving relevance and capacity to make a difference. A third is inclusivity; whether through partnerships, consortia, approaches or methods; enabling development studies to attend to the voices and perspectives of marginalised people. Finally, all this involves ongoing attention to power relations, along with humility and the questioning of one's own position and assumptions. None of this is easy, and the practices of development studies, as well as its scope and areas of focus, are constantly evolving. This makes it an endlessly difficult and dynamic, as well as an exciting field, as befits one grappling with the biggest challenges of our time. May this book find its place as a contribution to these challenges!

July 2021

Professor Melissa Leach CBE FBA
Director
Institute of Development Studies (IDS)
Sussex, UK

ACKNOWLEDGEMENTS

"I am not as good, as I want to be; as great as one day, I will be; but thanks to God, I am; so much better than I used to be"

(*Anonymous*)

The journey of writing this book has been as challenging for me as it has been amazing at the same time. The book in its present form has benefitted from many invaluable contributions. Though words may not be enough to express my gratitude, yet I would like to sincerely thank all of them.

First and foremost, I am grateful to Government of India for nominating me for the Masters program in Development Studies at the IDS, Sussex, UK, where most parts of this book were written. I am also grateful to Government of Maharashtra for allowing me to pursue this Masters program with timely relieving and requisite support. Institute of Development Studies (IDS) with University of Sussex, UK is inarguably the best institution in the world for the discipline of Development Studies. The QS University Rankings 2021 have ranked IDS, Sussex, first in the world for development studies (for the fifth year running), and it has been an absolute privilege and honor for me to be the alumni of this great institution. IDS has been instrumental in motivating me to follow my academic pursuit and fulfil my research capability in writing this book.

I warmly acknowledge and thank Prof. Melissa Leach, Director, IDS and one of the foremost thinkers on sustainability and development concerns in policy-making, for agreeing to write the foreword to this book as a short write up on 'Development – disruptions, definitions and debate'. The foreword aptly reflects the dynamism of development studies as reflected in this book. I thank Prof. Martin Greeley, Fellow, IDS and one of the leading development economists, for permitting me to use one of his figures as Figure 1.1 in this book. I also acknowledge the academic supervisors at the IDS for their insights and feedback on my essays. I am thankful to all authors and researchers referred to in this book as secondary sources. It has been a pleasure to work with Orient BlackSwan, and the cooperation of editorial and production staff is much appreciated.

My parents and parents-in-law have been unconditional source of support and comfort during the writing of this book, as they have always been. I specially mention my children Miss Veruschka and Master Parthsarthi, for being ever proud of me, never complaining about me giving their share of time and attention to my book, filling my life with joy and always pepping me up during the arduous journey of this book. My wife Seema has been by my side throughout, and if not for her, I would not have had the courage to embark on this journey. She challenges me to put my academic best in my research, readings and writings, helping me stick to my time commitments. Coping with the pressure which I bring home every day is not easy, but she handles it without any complaints, providing the much-needed sanity and anchoring in my life. I dedicate this first book of mine to her.

INTRODUCTION

> 'Our biggest challenge in this new century is to take an idea that seems abstract – sustainable development – and turn it into a reality for all the world's people.'
>
> – Kofi Annan*

It was a pleasant late morning of the famous English Autumn in first week of October 2019. I was immersed in the surreal natural beauty of South Downs visible from the French windows of my classroom at the Institute of Development Studies (IDS) during a short break. The class discussion was on the perspectives of development. Having already served in the Indian Administrative Service for over fourteen years in various capacities in rural and urban development at various places in Maharashtra, I had experienced development processes first hand as an administrator and practitioner of development. And here I was, trying to put in place the missing links between development practice and development theory, in my quest to gain insights into the development puzzle during my Masters program in Development Studies at the IDS, Sussex.

* Kofi Annan, the Secretary General of the United Nations, made this statement during his visit to Bangladesh on 15 March 2001. This visit was undertaken to further sustainable development agenda of the UN, throwing the moral authority of the UN behind the green development movement. The visit and this statement was widely covered in international media and received tremendous international attention. https://www.theguardian.com/environment/2001/mar/15/globalwarming.climatechange

The development initiatives, of which I had been a part of, during my service so far in the IAS, were coming to my mind. As I tried to look out for horizon over the sprawling South Downs, a thought flashed in my mind – Is India ever going to remain developing or will it ever be developed at some point of time?

Since her independence, India has undertaken an ambitious journey of development to become a developed nation, developing in the process, achieving milestones, aspiring for more ambitious milestones, achieving them too and so on. I soon realised that this question pretty much applies to all the developing countries. This cycle of development seemed to go on and on for developing countries, about 72 years for India now. If size of economy is the criterion, India would soon become world's fifth largest, replacing the United Kingdom. If political system is a criterion, India is world's largest stable democracy in the world. This was indeed intriguing for me, and I was sure, this would be a case for many others from the developing countries. It was at this point at the IDS, that I decided to devote my Masters program to find some clues to this development puzzle. This was the primary reason that most of my research at the IDS was India-centric, trying to find links between development theory and practice. During my stint at the IDS, I wrote eight academic papers – seven term-end and one off-term, on various themes of development, most of them involving India's varied development experiences, insights into these experiences and their introspection. These papers have dealt with both the development theory and development practice point of view. This book is a compilation of these academic papers.

The economists world over are divided over the issue of 'developing country' and 'developed country' tag, especially in case of big emerging economies like India. One way of looking at it is in terms of trade benefits that developing countries enjoy, while the other is to take into account the per capita income and human development indices, where countries like India have made tremendous progress but still lag behind the developed countries. Western developed economies led by the USA have been demanding to review the developing country status of India in international bodies like the World Trade Organisation and the World Bank. A developing country tag provides a leeway to provide more input subsidies and minimum support prices (MSP), and attracts lower tariffs and a longer timeline to implement the common global agenda. But this would be a skewed view keeping in mind that per capita income of the USA is over 30 times more than that of India. In fact, in February 2020, the USA has removed India from the list of developing economies and reclassified India as a developed economy for trade purposes.

Another important issue arising in the development debate is whether there is any time frame or time limit for a developing country to become developed. This is often linked to demographic dividend which countries like India have to their advantage. A State Bank of India study published in June 2018 mentioned that India has only one decade to become a developed nation before its demographic dividend turns into a demographic disadvantage by 2030. The report also stated that missing this time window would mean a risk of India staying a perpetually developing economy than becoming a developed one. With the dependency ratio of around 50%, India has a massive working age population to its advantage, before the old age population starts to catch up due to increased longevity and better healthcare facilities. As per the annual UN Human Development Reports, India took almost a decade of progress to move from low human development category in 2007 to medium category in 2017, when it ranked 131 out of 188 countries. At the same rate, it might take another decade or so for the country to move to high human development category and similar time to finally move to top level of very high human development category.

About a fourth of India's GDP comes from agriculture and allied sectors, the corresponding figure of developed economies being around 2%. Lately, developing economies like India have been denied concessional loans from multilateral donors due to high purchasing power parity (PPP). This is ironic, because, though India is still 'developing' in terms of GDP per capita, yet it is 'developed' enough in terms of PPP. This, in simple terms means that, India may be a low-income country, but prices of essential goods are low enough for the population to manage. This is a highly skewed method of evaluating development status of any country. The Western parameters of development have been derived largely based on experience of the Western industrialised economies, but what is seldom emphasised in development debate is that these countries have achieved the present levels of development in over 200 years post-industrialisation, which developing countries are expected to achieve in less than one third of time. For developing economies to cross over to developed club, it becomes imperative that they must not only grow, but grow faster than their developed counterparts. This has led to a thinking in development academia whether it is just and prudent to apply same set of development indices and metrics for developing countries.

All countries essentially started as developing countries to begin with; some of them eventually became developed and then devised the development criteria for the developing others. Famous British economist historian Angus Maddison estimated that in 1000 AD, India and China contributed to 50% of global GDP. Till about 1750 AD, India was one of the largest economies in the world, contributing around 25% of global GDP. By year 2020, India remains a third world country, with around 3% of global GDP, yearning from being developing to developed. It seems that development journey is getting prolonged for India with the years. On the other hand, Western economies, once classified as developed, continue to remain developed. But are the developed countries developed in true sense? This question needs to be answered on multiple parameters. One such potential parameter which is pivotal for a peaceful and progressive growth is the crime rate in society. A developed country like the USA has a crime rate which is more than that in many developing countries. Another potential parameter could be unemployment rate. Here also, the developed Western economies have been witnessing rising unemployment rates. During the course of my Masters Program at the IDS, it was a revelation to find that one of the critical civic issues faced by cities like London and Brighton is the rising number of homeless people over last few years. This points to context-specific issues in development. Is it fair to use the same gauge for measuring development in different contexts?

For a country like India, it is important to draw some development lessons from the history, especially the skill and knowledge-based economy derived through educated population and promotion of micro and small units of production, which led it to become world leader in GDP for about two centuries before it was colonised by the British. The quintessential Gandhian philosophy of holistic development essentially relates to the humane face of development, wherein the *Daridranarayan* – the poorest of the poor, is of utmost importance. UNDP refers to this poor population as the base of the pyramid, and Prahlad mentions it as the proverbial bottom of the pyramid. The objectives of Gandhian development include human development for capability expansion, balanced development through manual and intellectual workforce, development with social justice, rights and freedom, self-sufficiency and self-reliance of rural population through rural development, and poverty reduction through generation of additional income and employment. Gandhi aimed at what we have started referring to as sustainable development. Such development is not merely economic, but also social and moral. The emphasis of such development process is on decentralisation, community based economic growth, self-sufficiency, rural development, art, artisans and handicrafts, and low capital-intensive technology to achieve a sustainable growth.

India since independence, has undertaken a multitude of composite policy initiatives in its quest for development. These initiatives have attempted to address specific aspects of multi-dimensional concept of development, which India as a country is aspiring to achieve. Most of these efforts have been aimed at attaining small and targeted goals of development, playing complementary roles in reaching desired development milestones. All along, India's policy planning has been evolving though. To start with, Indian adopted an inward-looking development strategy post-independence, wherein the primary goal was to achieve industrial self-reliance and import substitution as a Non-Aligned nation. In late 1960s, this strategy was widened to include technological self-reliance and self-sufficiency in food grains production. In mid 1980s, this prolonged protectionist policy regime led to slow down of economic growth, wherein the country was branded by development theorists as having a 'Hindu rate of growth'. This led to a rethinking about the inward-looking policy though the attempts to move away from such a regime were sporadic and feeble. The 1990s witnessed a paradigm shift in this view of development when, facing a critical balance of payment crisis, India adopted structural and economic reforms and opened up its economy to the world, better known as the policy of liberalisation, privatisation and globalisation in common parlance.

India's development journey since 2000s has been largely based on its knowledge resources, with an emphasis on boosting productivity and gradually emerge as a knowledge economy. But here is a limitation – whereas India has been successful to emerge as a provider of lower-end activities (coding, process development, back-end support etc.) of high-tech sectors, it is still emerging as a provider of high-end activities (such as creating new technologies) of such sectors. This is usually referred to as the 'Indian model of development' in the development circles. Another peculiarity of this model is agriculture-dominated economy rather than manufacturing and processing-based one. Whereas almost a third of India's middle class urban, semi-urban and peri-urban population has benefitted from this development model, the challenges of health, nutrition, education and housing for the bottom fifth of rural population and those in urban slums still exist. Multilateral agencies' prescribed fiscal reforms mandate a reduction in public expenditure, therefore, it is imperative that the social sector, which is an invariable soft target for expenditure compression, gets its budgetary due, directly benefitting the bottom of the pyramid in true sense. In order to leapfrog its growth in its quest to become a developed country, India would need to adopt more of the market and more of the state, more state to retain the liberal democracy that is its hallmark; and more market to move away from extensive state ownership.

I would now come back to the present book. Each academic paper I wrote during my Masters program at the IDS has been presented as a chapter here. I have done minor alterations though, not in content per se, but in the appearance, so as to give a makeover to each paper as a book chapter. These papers have been written over a period of one year in 2019–20, under the academic supervision of IDS faculty, whom I duly acknowledge. On a cursory glance, the chapters might seem to be content-intense and concise, but the readers would need to bear the fact that these papers have been written in a strict word-limit format, which is unique to English higher education system, and any spillages attract heavy penalties in terms of academic grades awarded. While planning the content of this volume, I had consciously decided to maintain the current flow of content, and therefore had decided against adding any more material to these papers. This would also help avoid any dilution in the specific theme of each chapter from the perspective of keen readers.

This book is aptly titled '*Development: Experiences, Insights and Introspection*'. The variety of development themes included in this book represents the diversity of development experiences of India and other developing countries to an extent. These development themes range from pro-poor growth, pro-poor aid, international finance, public financial management, government as a development actor, market failure, India's development cooperation to South-South Cooperation and India's aid policy. This book touches upon the insights into the development experiences included and the learnings from these experiences, which can be applied to similar development processes in similar contextual settings. While doing so, this book tries to highlight more than seven decades of India's development journey. It also makes an attempt to look at the development process through different lenses – historical, social, economic, political, financial and administrative. I sincerely hope this book is well received by the development academicians and practitioners alike.

I

PRO-POOR GROWTH

MGNREGA and Poverty Reduction in India

Since the 1990s, the term "pro-poor growth" has evinced considerable interest and discussion within development community. But, a commonly agreed definition of pro-poor growth still remains at large. The global development goal has widened its focus from poverty reduction to pro-poor growth (Kakwani & Pernia, 2000). Various development experts have put in their own ideas of pro-poor growth, its dimensions and methodology to measure it, leading to definitional debate (Lopez, 2004). Literally, pro-poor growth is the growth which is good for poor. The concept of pro-poor growth in the existing development literature can be summed up in two broad categories, depending on whether the focus in on poverty outcomes or inequality outcomes (Lopez, 2004), or as the Department for International Development (DFID) has put it, absolute definitions (income centric) and relative definitions (comparative income centric with nonpoor) (DFID Policy Division, 2004). This paper attempts to discuss these different definitions, and dimensions, of pro-poor growth to address this definitional debate. It also reviews in brief the alternative approaches to measuring the pro-poor growth. Then, it discusses the Mahatma Gandhi National Rural Employment Guarantee Scheme (MGNREGS), as a case study, to explain its success in poverty reduction in India.

Pro-poor growth is about poverty reduction and improved well-being of the poor. Amartya Sen has conceptualised human well-being as functionings and capabilities, functionings as achievements and capabilities as the achieving ability. Thus, functionings relate to the actual life of people and capabilities as the freedom in the choosing functionings (Sen, 1987, p. 16). The concept of pro-poor growth has been intrinsic in the broad-based growth mentioned in the World Development Report, 1990 (The World Bank, 1990). Pro-poor growth is the inclusive growth which provides for the poor to engage in and gain considerably from economic activities, with the philosophy that no one is deprived of minimum capabilities (Kakwani & Pernia, 2000). Growth which results in more poverty fall, if incomes (for both poor and nonpoor) grow at the same rate[1] is the pro-poor growth (Baulch & McCulloch, 2000). Ravallion and Chen (2003) simply define pro-poor growth in terms of growth that reduces poverty. Kakwani and Pernia (2000) view the pro-poor growth as a major shift from traditional economic trickle-down approach and have also advanced it as a solution to the classical issue of efficiency-equity trade off.[2] Pro-poor growth which includes pro-poor policies and and pro-poor institutions promotes both equity and efficiency (Pernia & Quibria, 1999).

Lopez (2004) has explored the various factors affecting poverty and their interrelationship. The factors considered are growth of income and changes in income distribution and their relationship to changes in poverty, relationship between growth and inequality and whether growth results in less inequality, and how appropriate policies are related to the poverty reduction and reduction in inequalities (Lopez, 2004). He has suggested a common framework of these potential interacting factors to put the way forward for pro-poor growth.

Dollar and Kraay have analysed the effect of per capita GDP growth and income of the poor in a four-decade sample of 80 countries (Dollar & Kraay, 2000) and have shown that though growth generally has benefitted the poor, but has not affected the relative inequality much.[3] Kraay has identified three features of pro-poor growth as high rate of growth, more responsiveness of poverty to growth and growth having poverty reducing pattern (Kraay, 2004). He further suggests that a sensitive pro-poor growth strategy has to focus not only on growth, but also the growth pattern (meaning thereby, the beneficiaries of that growth). But, relative importance of these elements is still not conclusive.

While exploring the link between growth with equality (pro-poor growth) and poverty reduction, Eastwood and Lipton have put forth various dimensions of pro-poor growth. These include whether the growth is always or usually pro-poor, whether more growth is more pro-poor than less growth and whether equality is important to get pro-poor growth (Eastwood & Lipton, 2000). It has been shown that growth is more strongly pro-poor when initial inequality level is low, as in East Asia and South-East Asia, as against when initial inequality is high, as in Latin America (de Janury & Sadoulet, 2000). Also, labour-intensive agricultural growth may be better than industrial growth in being pro-poor (Timmer, 1997). Explaining the dimensions of pro-poor growth, Eastwood and Lipton (2000) have argued that pro-poor growth is closely linked to pro-growth poverty alleviation. Growth affects poverty in the same way as poverty affects growth. This mutual effect of growth on poverty and that of poverty on growth is cumulative and reinforcing. This means that a little pro-poor growth undergoes amplification as it reduces poverty; this in turn fuels further growth and so on. But if the growth is not pro-poor, it does not lead to poverty reduction and fails to result in more growth. Thus, whether growth results in poverty reduction and whether poverty reduction leads to more growth would depend on whether the growth is pro-poor or not.[4]

Kakwani and Pernia hold that market forces led growth is usually disproportionally beneficial to the rich vis-à-vis the poor. This is because the poor lack the human and material capital required to gain form such growth. This type of growth maintains and widens the inequalities between the rich and the poor. Pro-poor growth involves government policies[5] and growth strategies which benefit poor more due to pro-poor bias. This not only reduces overall poverty, but also reduces the inequalities (Kakwani & Pernia, 2000). Eastwood and Lipton suggest that labour-intensive growth in the production of staple foods on small-scale farms and incentivising fertility reduction in poor[6] can result in achieving pro-poor growth. High agriculture growth rate is linked to reduction in poverty subsequently. Also, declining fertility results in faster per capita GDP and consumption growth, resulting in poverty reduction (Eastwood & Lipton, 2000).

As I have discussed so far, human well-being is multi-dimensional, so is the pro-poor growth. This poses challenges in measurement of pro-poor growth. McCulloch and Baulch (1999) at the Institute of Development Studies (IDS), Sussex, have attempted a simple operational definition of pro-poor growth employing 'poverty bias of growth'.[7] Using data from Indian States of Andhra Pradesh and Uttar Pradesh, they demonstrated that poverty reduction is a factor of both the economic growth rate and income distribution changes (McCulloch & Baulch, 1999). Hyun Hwa Son (2004) has proposed a 'poverty growth curve' for measuring pro-poor economic growth by using household survey data of Thailand and cross-country international data. This curve is modelled along the lines of Lorenz curve.[8]

Martin Greeley has detailed the the multi-dimensional nature of poverty and well-being in context of poverty reduction and pro-poor growth policies and strategies. According to him, the vulnerablities like gender, age, disability, ethnicity, caste, family size lead to poverty and so do the shocks the poor face in form of economic crises, conflict, diseases, floods and droughts. Vulnerabilites and shocks reinforce poverty in the poor. Income growth, assets creation and availability of essential services lead to empowerment of poor out of vicious cycle of poverty, aptly addressed as the pro-poor growth (Greeley, 2019).

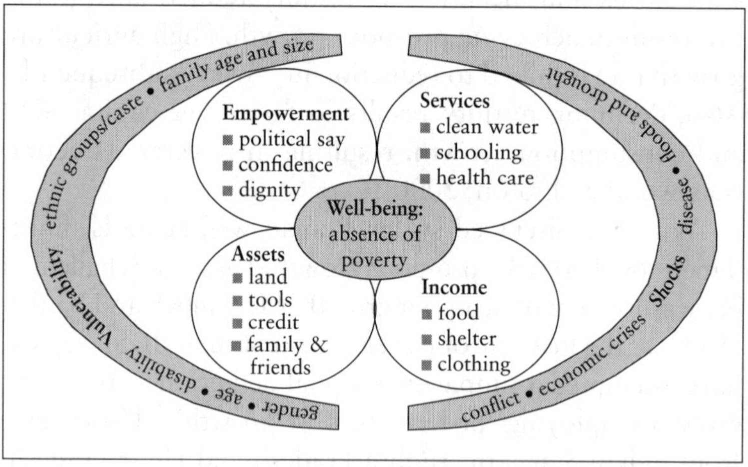

Figure 1.1: Dimensions of poverty and well-being (Greeley, 2019).

Mahatma Gandhi National Rural Employment Guarantee Act (MGNREGA): A case study of success in poverty reduction in India

National Rural Employment Guarantee Act (NREGA) was enacted as a Central Legislation in September 2005 to enhance livelihood security of the poor rural households by providing minimum one hundred days of guaranteed wage employment to every poor household whose adult members volunteered to do unskilled manual work (Government of India, 2005). NREGA was launched in February 2006 and national coverage of the program was completed in October 2007. It was renamed as the Mahatma Gandhi National Rural Employment Guarantee Act (MGNREGA) in October 2008. MGNREGA is a Government of India program with a unique participatory planning process at the grassroot level of democracy – the Gram Sabha (village assembly) at the village level. It is a demand-driven, rights-based program of locally selected works and their execution (Desai, Vashishtha, & Joshi, 2015). MGNREGA provides for legally guaranteed employment, statutory minimum wage, unemployment allowance (if employment is not made available within 15 days of demand), bottom-up participatory planning, sustainable rural assets creation and long-term livelihood opportunities to rural poor. As World Bank has put it, involving more than 50 million beneficiary households and annual expenditure ranging from 0.5% to 1% of the GDP, MGNREGA is one of the largest anti-poverty programs in the world (World Bank Group, 2015).

Various researchers have attempted to assess the success of MGNREGA in terms of reduction of poverty in India.

Though conceptualised as a wage-employment program to supplement the income of rural poor, particularly in lean agricultural season, MGNREGA has been shown to have far-reaching socio-economic consequences in rural beneficiary households, the primary one being the reduction of poverty (World Bank Group, 2015). The World Bank report on India Development Update has discussed how MGNREGA has led to poverty reduction in India. MGNREGA reduces poverty directly by making available extra employment and income opportunity to the rural poor and by creating assets of value for poor e.g., irrigation ponds. Further, the program also has indirect effect on poverty reduction as it generates further employment through infrastructural assets creation e.g., rural roads. Another indirect effect of MGNREGA on poverty reduction has been due to improved rural wage structure. Reduced dependence on moneylenders, reduced incidence of child labour and improvement in school years for the rural children are few of the other indirect ways in which MGNREGA has helped in reduction of rural poverty (World Bank Group, 2015).

MGNREGA has perceptible multiplier effects on socio-economic development, apart from reduction in poverty by providing predictable and assured subsistence wage, enlargement of consumption basket due to enhanced income, gender equity, better natural resource management, better wages and more purchasing power for the rural poor, deepening democracy by inclusion and participation leading to rural poor empowerment (United Nations Development Programme, 2010, p. 53).

Sarkar, Kumar, & Supriya (2011) have studied the socio-econonic effect of MGNREGA on rural poor in Burdwan district of West Bengal. They have reported significant positive outcomes in the socio-economic variables for the beneficiary

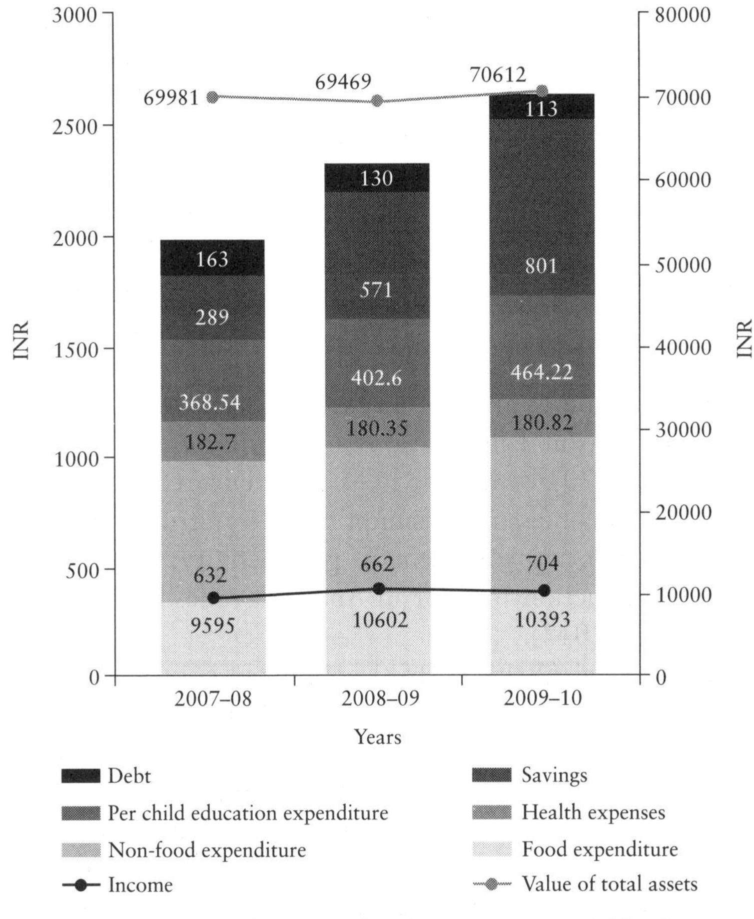

Figure 1.2: Yearly value of socio-economic variables for MGNREGA beneficiary households (Adapted from Sarkar, Kumar, & Supriya, 2011). All figures are in per capita INR and annual, except food expenditure, which is monthly.

households. These variables, among others, include per capita income. A socio-economic index[9] was prepared and the study showed that, from 2007–08 to 2008–09, the percentage of beneficiary households in poor socio-economic conditions witnessed a reduction from 43.9% to 32.9%, and further to 18.3% in 2009–10. The study strongly supports the success of MGNREGA in poverty reduction in beneficiary households. These findings are shown in Figure 1.2.

Similar positive outcomes of MGNREGA on rural household consumption and rural poverty rates have been reported by Klonner & Oldiges (2014) supporting the success of MGNREGA in poverty reduction. They found that rural agricultural labourers experience reduction in poverty by as much as 50% during the lean farming season. Also, MGNREGA has stabilised the consumption pattern[10] in the target population across agricultural seasons by reducing seasonal fluctuations in consumption (Klonner & Oldiges, 2014). MGNREGA has delivered significant positive outcomes in consumption and nutrition patters, asset quality, improvement in productivity; apart from poverty reduction in poor in Andhra Pradesh (Deininger & Yanyan, 2013).

Dutta et al (2014, p. 158) conducted survey of 2,700 rural households in Bihar in two rounds in 2009 and 2010. The analysis of data puts forth that in ideal conditions, with MGNREGA intervention, the rural poverty rate[11] of 50% at the beginning of survey could reduce by at least 14 percentage points. This study goes to show the success of MGNREGA in poverty reduction in Bihar. The role of

Table 1.1: Percentage of Below Poverty Line (BPL) households (Dutta, Murgai, Ravallion, & van de Walle, 2014)

Stage	Survey Round I	Survey Round II
Year	2009	2010
Pre-MGNREGA intervention	62.2%	52.6%
Post-MGNREGA intervention	56.8%	50.2%
Reduction in poverty	5.4%	2.4%

MGNREGA in reducing beneficiary household poverty has been shown in Table 1.1.

Desai, Vashishtha, & Joshi (2015, p. 60) have perused the MGNREGA performance data from MGNREGA annual reports from year 2006–07 till 2013–14. The salient findings of their report strongly indicate towards the success of MGNREGA in poverty reduction in India. The report finds that MGNREGA has caused poverty reduction up to 32% overall and prevented 14 million rural population from slipping into poverty. This has been possible because the program is non-discriminatory and equal opportunity provider, and reinforces the incomes of the poor[12] when there is no other source of income available for them, such as, in lean farm season. Further, in 2004–05, almost 45% of female participants in MGNREGA were those who never worked in farms or those who worked as farm wage labourers. This shows that MGNREGA emerged as the first opportunity for such female participants to earn cash incomes, outside of farm wages. Similarly, rural poor and socially vulnerable farm labourers, tribals, backward class poor, small and marginal

Table 1.2: Impact of MGNREGA on poverty reduction (Desai, Vashishtha, & Joshi, 2015)

Categories	Poverty ratio 2004–05 (%)	Poverty ratio 2011–12 (%)	Decline in poverty (%)	Contribution of MGNREGA to poverty reduction (%)
MGNREGA participants overall	52.2	31.3	20.9	32.1
Scheduled tribes	54.3	33.8	20.5	37.6
Scheduled castes	75.8	45.7	30.1	27.6
Illiterate workers	58.9	36.4	22.5	35.6

farmers have been benefitted across India by MGNREGA. The results have been summed up and shown in Table 1.2.

Institute of Economic Growth (IEG) has conducted a survey[13] of 30 selected districts across India to study the income impact of MGNREGA in the beneficiary households. It has been found that household income increased in all selected districts and gross annual income per household of all 30 districts taken together show a growth of 11.1% form 2015–16 to 2016–17, a span of two years (Institute of Economic Growth, 2018). The results have been shown in Table 1.3 below.

Table 1.3: Average income growth of beneficiaries in 30 districts covered (IEG 2018, p. 41)

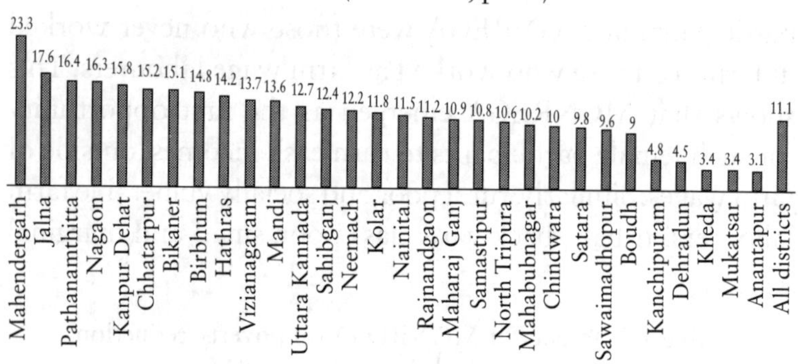

Thus, the foregoing discussion makes it amply clear that MGNREGA emerges as a case study of success in reducing poverty in India. Therefore, it has assumed importance in the poverty alleviation strategy and policies of the country. Successive governments have acknowledged the poverty reduction potential of MGNREGA; this is evident from the fact that MGNREGA continues to enjoy healthy budgetary allocation in respective Union budgets since its launch in 2004–05. Coupled with its reach in the poor population and pro-poor outlook, MGNREGA has been a gamechanger in the rural economy and rural poverty. The pro-poor growth approach of MGNREGA has ensured that the rural poor not only get more incomes, but there is also more equitable distribution of these incomes.

Notes

1. The distributional shift happens in the pro-poor growth process wherein the incomes of the poor increase at a greater rate than the nonpoor with the same growth rate.

2. Pernia and Quibria (1999) point out that removal of anti-poor institutional limitations and biases in policies might improve market efficiency and promote equity. Similarly, social policy involving adequate education and healthcare to the poor would improve their productivity and economic contribution.

3. Though Dollar and Kraay put forth a strong argument, the conclusions are not convincing because of inconsistency in measurement of income, inequality and poverty across countries and individual country experiences can vary significantly.

4. It is usually difficult to prove pro-poor growth by data analysis. Moreover, data analysis cannot firmly establish pro-growth poverty reduction because most growth spells are short-lived, making it difficult for the researchers to interpret tests of causation for pro-growth poverty reduction.

5. Pro-poor policies include macro policies such as industrial location policies, micro policies such as subsidised public utilities like water and electricity; and direct pro-poor policies such as increased public expenditure on health, education and family planning services and progressive taxation policy.

6. Reduced fertility would lead to reduced child mortality, increased options of better education, work and family planning information for the females in the poor population further causing decline in fertility.

7. The poverty bias of growth is calculated by reducing changes in poverty headcount that took place between any two periods in actual circumstances from the change in poverty which would happen if all gain equally. The poverty headcount ratio is defined as the proportion of the population with income or consumption expenditure below the poverty threshold (national poverty line or Dollar poverty line).

8. As Kakwani and Pernia (2000) hold, pro-poor growth benefits poor population more than the nonpoor population. So, inequality declines in pro-poor growth. A change in Lorenz curve shows this effect. If the curve shifts upwards, growth is labelled pro-poor.

9. The socio-economic index consists of 12 variables – annual per capita income, monthly per capita food expenditure, annual per capita non-food expenditure, per capita productive assets, possession of other assets, condition of dwelling house, rooms per person, annual per child education expenditure, annual per capita healthcare expenditure, access to healthcare facilities, per capita savings and per capita outstanding debt.

10. Klonner and Oldiges have combined regionally coded data of consumption surveys with information on district-wise rollout of MGNREGA. They have estimated the effect of MGNREGA on poverty reduction by employing a regression discontinuity design.

11. To estimate poverty, the researchers have used median per capita consumption (PCC) level from Survey Round I and updated it during the study period with consumer price index to get the Survey Round II figures.

12. Among the rural population, 30% of poor households worked in MGNREGA across the country as against 21% of nonpoor households. These findings are also an indirect indication of poverty reducing capability of MGNREGA, and this is instrumental in drawing poor households to participate in the MGNREGA.

13. IEG surveyed 30 rural districts in 21 states involving a total of 1,200 beneficiary households (40 from each district). The selection of districts was based on natural resource management expenditure per MGNREGA worker.

II

ECONOMIC GROWTH MATTERS, BUT SO DOES PRO-POOR GROWTH AGENDA OF DONORS

United Nations Development Programme (UNDP) has identified economic growth as a crucial factor in both development and underdevelopment. Since the 1950s, the central tenet of economic growth has moved from mere 'trickle down' to 'growth with development' in 2000s. Development includes major transformation of society in terms of economic, social and institutional areas leading to long-term, paced and patterned poverty reduction in such societies. This paper attempts to present the viewpoint of pro-poor growth to address multi-dimensional poverty in the donors' quest for development and growth in the aid recipient countries. To start with, I discuss the paradigm shifts in the theme of economic growth from 1950s to 2000s, and how this has become more centric to poverty reduction strategies in poor countries. To set the theoretical context of the paper, I discuss about pro-poor growth and its importance in poverty reduction. I dwell on the DAC guidelines to further elaborate the concept of development cooperation and pro-poor growth agenda of the donors. I then discuss how the traditional aid recipes based on "our solutions to their problems", "business as usual" agenda and "more of the same" is not sufficient for pro-poor growth in the partner countries. Based on this construct, I then elaborate how the pro-poor growth agenda of the donors can be implemented in furthering the cause of poverty reduction in aid recipient countries. Then I make a passing reference to the case of Liberia, a coastal West African low-income nation, to emphasise how pro-poor growth agenda of the foreign aid has been impacting the poverty reduction efforts in Liberia since last decade. I sum up by mentioning that it is imperative that the aid recipient countries keep pushing for strong donor support for national policy reforms and capacity building to emerge as a successful case of pro-poor growth agenda of the donors with strong and consistent aid flow to reduce poverty in long-term.

Economic growth and development

Economic growth is a crucial factor in development and also in underdevelopment (United Nations Development Programme, 1994). The last five decades have witnessed phenomenal growth and prosperity in the world, but this has happened in certain regions and further in certain countries within those regions. Thus, some countries have remained stagnant and even deteriorated further in terms of economic growth. In 1950s and 1960s, the development theories revolved around the central tenet of 'trickle down', wherein it was assumed that economic growth and development would trickle down from successful areas to more peripheral underdeveloped areas, resulting in the catching up by the marginalised areas with the growth trajectory of developed areas (Kingsbury, Remenyi, Mckay, Hunt, & Buchy, 2004). These modernization theories also guided the central perception of the Bretton Woods Institutions – the World Bank and the International Monetary Fund. The trickle-down theory came to be challenged by the 'dependency school' arguments in the 1960s, when it was reported that as the North became increasingly prosperous, the South became more impoverished. Also, the idea that development meant modernization as in Westernization was contested (Seers, 1969).

Since the end of Cold War, the 'neo dependency school' of development has emerged which impinges on liberal democracy as the 'only viable economic and political system in the modern world' (Kingsbury, Remenyi, Mckay, Hunt, & Buchy, 2004) to achieve economic growth and development. But since then, the 'correct policies' approach to development is being increasingly argued against (Rivero, 2001). Since 1990s, there has been much discussion in the realm of development policy about the mutually reinforcing processes of poverty, resulting due to lack of economic growth, and the underdevelopment. It has been argued that poverty leads to poor savings, resulting in insufficient investment and eventually low or no economic growth and development.

In the 2000s, globalisation has become the pivot of the development debate. Globalisation has been referred to include increased transnational economic activities, more and more international economic integration and reforms, leading to economic growth and development (Robson, 1984). This has been referred to as the newer version of modernization theory of economic growth and development. In the era of globalization, every country is in the pursuit of development. Economic growth coupled with economic progress is an essential component of development, but it is not the only component, as development is not purely economic phenomenon (Todaro & Smith, 2009). It typically involves modification in institutional, social and administrative systems and structures as well.

The relationship between economic growth and development has been examined by Paul Rosenstein-Rodan while pioneering the 'big push model' of development.

The big push model explains how market failures result in the need of public economic policy to usher in economic development and successful industrialisation. The model further explains that for this to happen, neither the private players nor the state plays the role of super entrepreneur, rather public coordination of private actions is required (Rosenstein-Rodan, 1943). The industrial policies of East Asian nations are example of this.

The new economic view of development slowly emerged when it was reported that in the latter half of 20th century, many developing nations did achieve their economic growth targets in terms of absolute GDP growth, but the living standard of population of these nations remained the same. To explain this gap, Dudley Seers in 1969 came up with poverty, unemployment and income inequality as the central problems of the economic growth and development. He held that along with the economic growth of a country, if any of these central problems grew worse over time, then it would be strange to call the outcome as 'development' (Seers, 1969). Amartya Sen (2009) has further explained the idea of development by suggesting 'subjective well-being' of the person and her 'capability to function' in terms of choice of actions. He has differentiated 'growth with development', which emphasises on health, education, social inclusion and empowerment, from the 'growth without development', which is characterised typically by high income levels but poor health, education and inclusiveness. Further, he has suggested happiness as an important function of well-being of a person (Sen, 2009).

In the recent researches, Layard (2005) has explored the relationship between satisfaction and happiness with average income levels in various countries. He found that though the average happiness level increases with average income, this relationship is evident only up to certain average per capita income level of $10,000 to $12,000. Once this income level is achieved, it is the expanded human capabilities which result in increased happiness level. Thus, financial security and economic growth (economic capital) is only one factor affecting happiness, the other important factor being social capital (Layard, 2005).

United Nations Development Programme (UNDP) has identified the basic life-sustaining human needs as food, shelter, health and protection. 'Absolute under-development' exists when any of these needs is in critically short supply or absent. A basic function of all economic activity and economic growth is to overcome the lack of these basic human needs. To that extent, economic growth becomes a necessary condition for life quality improvement, that is, development (United Nations Development Programme, 1994). As Amartya Sen has also emphasised, realisation of human potential would not be possible without continuous and sustained economic growth. Rising per capita income, elimination of absolute poverty, greater employment opportunities and lessening income inequalities therefore constitute the 'necessary' but not the 'sufficient' conditions for development (Sen, 2009).

Thus, economic growth definitely ushers in efficient resource allocation and steady growth of economic output over time. This, coupled with social and institutional mechanisms, brings in rapid and large-scale improvement in living standard for the poor of developing nations by invoking appropriate public policies. This in turn results in major economic, institutional and social transformations of these societies, as a whole, called 'development'. Development therefore, is a product of an interdependent social system in which economic growth and non-economic forces continually interact, adding up to more than the sum of their parts, catalysed by the state policies (Todaro & Smith, 2009).

WHY PRO-POOR GROWTH MATTERS?

The causes of poverty extend beyond only economic dimension and include interlinked political, socio-cultural, human and security dimensions too. Pro-poor growth addresses these multiple and interlinked dimensions to reduce economic poverty (Organisation for Economic Cooperation and Development, 2007).

The experience of last five decades or so of developing countries in their dual quest of economic growth and poverty reduction has been far form satisfactory. Some

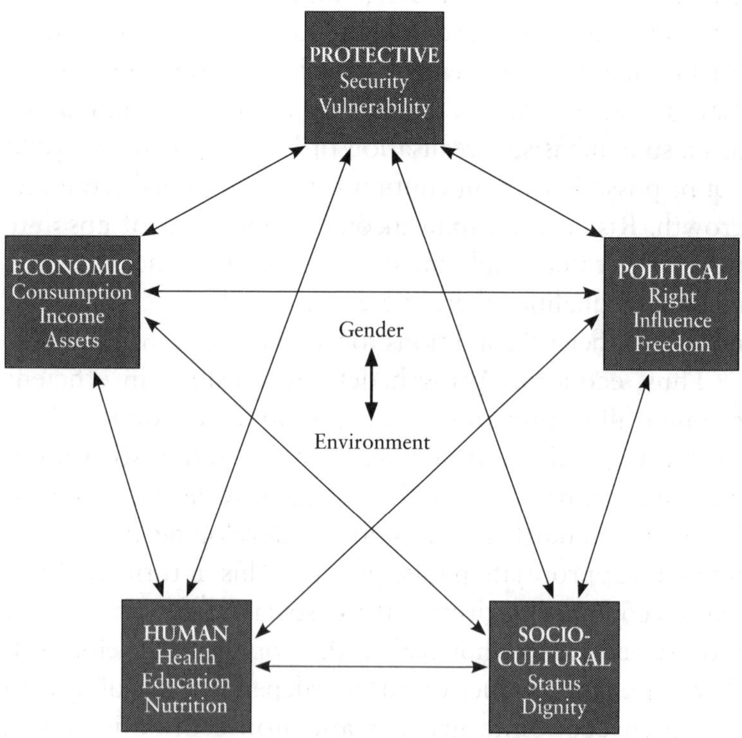

Figure 2.1: Interactive dimensions of poverty and well-being (Organisation for Economic Co-operation and Development, 2001)

countries like India and China have achieved some success in sustaining high growth rates and also have been able to pull out substantial portion of poor out of poverty. On the other hand, there are Latin American countries, which though have achieved higher economic growth rate, yet have not got much success in poverty reduction. Then there are Sub-Saharan countries, whose efforts have not met with proportionate success in either of the two areas. Even in the countries where overall performance for growth and poverty reduction has been satisfactory, this process has witnessed the marginalisation of significant portion of poor from the growth process (Mckay, 2005).

The concept of pro-poor growth can be theoretically explained in two ways – in absolute terms and in relative terms. The absolute view of pro-poor growth takes into account the absolute rate of growth of income of the poor, whereas the relative view focuses on relative income growth of poor vis-à-vis non-poor. From the point of view of sustained and rapid poverty reduction, both these views are relevant, because it is essential for growth to result in proportion income benefit for the poor relative to the non-poor (Klasen, 2005). There is a fair consensus among the development practitioners and thinkers that economic growth is an essential factor in poverty reduction. Faster the economic growth, faster is the effect on reducing income poverty. The experiences of 14 developing countries in the 1990s point to a direct relation between the rate of growth and the decline in poverty (AFD, 2005). But to sustain the pace of this poverty reduction effect, it is imperative to incentivise investment, increase the capital and labour productivity and positive business sentiment by way of institutional and policy interventions, as has been the case with the Indian experience of growth and poverty reduction since 1990s (Rodrik & Subramanian, 2004).

The Development Assistance Committee (DAC) guidelines on poverty reduction suggest three policy strategies to reduce poverty. First, pro-poor growth, which is inclusive, contributory and beneficial, leads to sustained and sustainable poverty reduction at a rapid pace and long-term growth. Second, mutually reinforcing poverty reduction policies cutting across various dimensions of poverty, with the absence of policy dichotomy, are needed to tackle poverty and usher in pro-poor growth. Third, such poverty reduction policies must be poor-centric and accountable to the poor, augmenting the economic activities to address multi-dimensional poverty and boost pro-poor growth (Organisation for Economic Co-operation and Development, 2001).

To elaborate further on the DAC guidelines, economic growth majorly contributes to poverty reduction, but for poverty reduction to be sustained and rapid, the pattern of such economic growth has to be inclusive and broadly cover all dimensions of poverty. Merely economic growth may not be that effective in reducing poverty, as is pro-poor growth with a clear focus on enabling conducive participation of the poor in such growth process. This is because pure economic growth leads to inequality of distribution by the very nature of market forces; on the contrary, pro-poor growth helps in achieving both income and distributional objectives of such growth. The bottom of the pyramid poor population is vulnerable and has extremely low risk taking and risk absorbing capacity, therefore, it is left out of high-risk growth opportunities. Pro-poor growth intends to address this issue of vulnerability and risk, leading to more inclusive growth opportunities for the poor. Further, poor have disadvantage in terms of market access and market participation, so, any market failure affects them disproportionately leading to further reduced economic capability. Pro-poor growth intends to provide well-functioning market, which is designed to avoid market failure and replacing such market failure, if it at all happens, with subsequent government failure (Organisation for Economic Co-operation and Development, 2001). Any poverty reduction strategies should be responsive, enabling and accountable to the poor to qualify as pro-poor growth strategies. This also implies the presence of a well-functioning state to provide policy framework and implementation machinery to usher in pro-poor growth.

Environmental sustainability has been increasing recognised as a vital ingredient for pro-poor growth. Coupled with effective governance and sound regulatory framework, this is what makes a state a well functional state capable of achieving pro-poor growth. Developing countries depend much more on their natural resources exploitation than developed ones, leading to resource curse (Sachs & Warner, 1995), meaning thereby that developing countries focus on natural resource-based growth policies rather than broad-based and multisectoral growth. The natural resources, in such countries, become the curse for sustained poverty rather than a basis of pro-poor growth.

Development cooperation and pro-poor growth agenda

Though one of the main roles of development cooperation is supposed to be poverty reduction in aid recipient countries, yet it is not possible to arrive at a universally applicable foreign aid prescription due to multitude of contextual settings in recipient countries in terms of variation in economic policies and growth, availability of natural resources and a well-functioning governance mechanism, and development policies and institutions (World Bank, 2005). Pure pro-growth oriented development cooperation prescribed by OECD in 1960s and 1970s in countries like Egypt and Brazil did result in increased growth rate due to this aid, but this growth rate was not sustainable as it left development of human capital out of the aid purview. It became increasingly evident that pro-growth development cooperation policies had to be pro-poor too (United Nations Development Programme, 1996). There is a broad consensus among donors now that economic growth and human development have to go side-by-side to sustain growth and reduce poverty in aid recipient countries, as the traditional dichotomy between pro-poor and pro-growth aid policies is blurring.

There may be trade-offs between pro-poor and pro-growth aid policies, but such trade-offs are observed in short term, when the initial choice between economic growth and human development is needed to be made by the aid recipients. Such trade-offs can be set off by employing the pro-poor growth lens to examine the current state of economy, poverty and inequality and then prioritising the focus areas accordingly. It is possible to address both pro-poor and pro-growth objectives of foreign aid by focusing on complementary policies, such as deepening micro-financing, which give a boost to both economic growth and pro-poor growth (Beck, Demirguc-Kunt, & Levine, 2004). Such an approach takes into account the interlinkages in various dimensions of poverty, the economic reality, and the social determinants of poverty to frame a comprehensive approach for poverty reduction in a particular aid recipient country. Such approach strives to be inclusive and representative to take care of the interests of poor and vulnerable in the implementation of such aid-driven poverty reduction program.

This forms the basis of the pro-poor growth agenda of the donors, which underlines the importance of addressing the recipient-specific constraints to pro-poor growth in unique contextual setting of that recipient country. The pro-poor growth agenda of donors also recognises the fact that the development cooperation experience in one contextual setting cannot be directly applied in a different setting, and that the traditional dichotomy between economic growth and human development (pro-poor growth) is misplaced (Organisation for Economic Co-operation and Development, 2001). The OECD identifies three central themes in the pro-poor growth agenda of the donors (Organisation for Economic Cooperation and Development, 2007). These are –

a) Providing "our solutions to their problems" is unproductive for sustained and rapid poverty reduction.
b) Pro-poor growth agenda of donors is not "Business as usual" agenda.
c) "More of the same" is not sufficient for the pro-poor growth.

a) "Our solutions to their problems"

The pro-poor growth agenda of donors acknowledges that providing "our solutions to their problems" does not work because pro-poor growth cannot be imposed externally on the recipient country, as also what has worked in one contextual setting would not work as such in another context. The Paris Declaration on Aid Effectiveness has laid down the guiding principles for donors for designing pro-poor growth in recipient partner countries. Any pro-poor aid program should be based on continuous broad-based consultative process between the donor and recipient partner, and should strengthen prevailing poverty reduction policies in relevant local context. An aid program designed on this basis identifies the context-specific innovations to tackle the constraints to pro-poor growth, rather than being based on donor prescription or donor priorities or donor experiences with other recipients (Organisation for Economic Co-operation and Development, 2005).

b) "Business as usual"

Development cooperation which is extended in routine as "business as usual" is not sufficient to achieve the pro-poor growth agenda. The pro-poor growth agenda is aimed at not merely advancing aid, but to bring about such institutional and policy changes which enable the poor to influence such pro-poor changes by their inclusion and participation. This means that the donors need to rework the rules of engagement and aid modalities with development partners, which is a clear divergence from the "business as usual" aid agenda. One of the key differences between usual aid agenda and pro-poor growth agenda lies in accepting the lead taken by the recipient partner to develop poverty reducing strategies based on the local conditions, and by involving the true beneficiaries of pro-poor growth in such policy changes. The donors should support such policy initiatives and include them in the designing of aid program so that the aid is better aligned to achieve pro-poor growth (Organisation for Economic Co-operation and Development, 2005).

c) "More of the same"

The Paris Declaration on Aid Effectiveness has shown that merely scaling up the aid quantum to reduce poverty in recipient country is not effective because "more of the same" is not sufficient for the pro-poor growth, as has been evident in the case of traditional aid experiences of 1970s and 1980s. Though it has been widely accepted that the donor intervention in terms of foreign aid has to be long-term, yet only its duration and quantum do not yield the desired pro-poor growth unless such aid is flexible and responsive to contextual settings. Thus, pro-poor growth agenda has to be necessarily long-term, continuous intervention, guided by the poverty and inequality experience of the partner country. For example, foreign aid program for middle-income countries needs to focus more on regional development imbalances, gender and social income imbalances and creating inclusive employment opportunities, whereas such aid program for low-income countries need to focus more on budgetary support so that the state remains functional, and does not become a failed state, so that implementation of poverty reduction strategies can be gradually introduced and taken up.

Implementation of the pro-poor growth agenda of the donors

The DAC has prescribed poverty and social impact analysis by the donors to analyse the impact of aid intervention on the distribution and welfare of poor and vulnerable in the recipient countries (Organisation for Economic Co-operation and Development, 2001). Such analysis essentially is possible using a pro-poor growth lens so that the areas having the greatest impact on pro-poor growth can be targeted by the pro-poor growth agenda of the donors. Such areas include private sector, infrastructure and agriculture, which have the capability for boosting pro-poor growth in the aid recipient countries, impacting both the pattern and the pace of such growth. Sustained and inclusive private sector development by way of foreign aid intervention needs certain policy shaping by such aid programs. Major areas of such policy outcomes are minimalizing administrative-regulatory barriers, encouraging competition by capacity building and promoting the supply-side response by providing a level playing market, providing greater access to financial services and support through formal finance and microfinance channels, improving gender access to labour, financial and services markets and providing an inclusive public-private engagement on sustained basis. Similar policy inputs in agriculture sector focus on improving market and credit access, facilitating non-farm income, risk mitigation strategies such as crop insurance and sustainable rural development planning.

Ushering in pro-poor growth agenda of donors require the aid program to support recipient led poverty reduction efforts in achieving pro-poor growth targets. This means the donors need to be flexible enough to delegate greater decision-making roles to the recipients based on local governance and contextual challenges and supportive of local solutions to such challenges for an extended period of time (Dahl-Ostergaard, 2005). Such aid program should demonstrate an understanding of how development interventions transmit and affect the poor and vulnerable during the course of such interventions. Continued and sustained focus on integration of political, social and economic opportunities, needs and perspectives would need re-orientation of such pro-poor growth agenda from time-to-time. This also means a total shift in the way such aid program is evaluated in terms of its effectiveness, from being aid-volume (input) based to impact and outcome based. Thus, there is a need to have aid program which is donor provided but locally owned, long-term and locally adapted, flexible in terms of dynamic needs of recipient, and commonly agreed in terms of best mix of interventions evolved during a sustainable and comprehensive donor-recipient dialogue in contextual settings, with a clear view of upholding rule of law and governance reforms in the recipient countries.

Liberia: A Case of Pro-Poor Growth Agenda of the Donors

Now, I briefly mention here the case of Liberia, a coastal West African low-income nation, to emphasise how a pro-poor agenda driven foreign aid has the potential of impacting the poverty reduction efforts of such recipients. Officially classified as a fragile state by the World Bank, its nearly two-decade civil war and Ebola epidemic of 2014–15 have pushed it deep into poverty and malnutrition. More than half of Liberia's population is classified as poor, with rural poverty at 71.6% (International Fund for Agricultural Development, 2019). Agriculture is the mainstay of rural development in Liberia, despite it being subsistence to a large extent. National spending on agriculture is less than 3% of total expenditure. Thus, Liberia depends on foreign aid for its funding needs in agriculture sector, most of which is in the form of grant. The aid seeks to augment public investment in rural development in Liberia over a long-term period to support sustainable and inclusive agriculture, gradually weaning it away from subsistence to commercial farming (Jalles d'Orey, 2020). Such aid is targeted at improving access to agricultural technologies and production services, agriculture value-chain development, basic rural infrastructure, risk-mitigation and climate resilience in agriculture and access to finance and microfinance services in rural areas in a favourable investment atmosphere suited to local needs. Within the Liberia's pro-poor aid agenda of the donors, the agricultural sector is recognised as being critical for poverty reduction and structural transformation of rural area (Prizzon, Chen, & Jalles d'Orey, 2020). The aid strives to target small and marginal farmers, including the poor and vulnerable women and youth engaged in such subsistence farming. In fact, from 2009 to 2018, the foreign aid component for agriculture and rural development sector in Liberia has more than doubled from 6% to 13.4%, reflecting the donors' commitment to this sector (Jalles d'Orey, 2020).

One of the key reasons for such a foreign aid program to be effective in impacting the agriculture sector in a recipient like Liberia has been identified as the alignment of aid program to the national and local needs and priorities of Liberia's rural development. Transparency and accountability in implementation of such aid program by the Liberian government as mandated by external development assistance has resulted in effective utilisation of such aid in development of rural sector in Liberia over the years of this aid flow. Coupled with the long-term and sustainable commitment of aid financing by the donors, responded ably with delivery speed and flexibility by the Liberian government, this aid program has responded well to emergency needs, likes of which were observed during recent Ebola crisis. The fact that over 98% of such aid funds have been disbursed as scheduled over last decade with high annual predictability of stable aid flow has also helped government of Liberia to evolve its agriculture and rural development policies in sync with such aid priorities. Liberia has consistently demanded a strong donor support for its policy reforms and capacity building, and a strong aid flow with consistency of aid design, policy and field action. This has propelled Liberia as a successful case of pro-poor growth agenda of the donors over the years, despite its fragility and enormous challenges in agriculture sector (United Nations Development Programme, 2020).

Conclusion

The pro-poor growth agenda of the donors has been prescribed by the DAC as a tool to target the desired outcome of foreign aid in recipient countries in terms of long-term, paced and patterned, sustainable and inclusive poverty reduction in both absolute and relative terms. For the donors, such agenda ensures that contextual settings are taken into consideration while framing and implementing such aid program. On the other hand, for the recipients, this effectively means a strong donor-driven policy reforms and capacity building, along with consistent and steady aid flow to effectively reduce poverty and achieve pro-poor growth targets. In this paper, I have given a context of economic growth, moving on to growth with development, pro-poor growth and pro-poor growth agenda of the donors for the aid recipient countries. I have explained how the pro-poor growth agenda of the donors matters for the recipients and how it is different from business-as-usual aid agenda. Then,

I have highlighted the important components of such pro-poor growth agenda of the donor aid in implementation of such aid program in the recipient countries, citing the case of Liberia briefly to drive home the point of contextual settings in such aid agenda. I have summed up by stating that for a successful pro-poor growth agenda led by foreign aid, it is important for both the donors and the recipients to commit to such agenda by continuous donor support and national policy reforms.

III

DEVELOPMENT TAKEAWAYS

Maximising Gains from International Finance

International finance has always been a topic of intense discussions in the development economists' community. East Asian financial crisis of 1990s and global financial crisis of 2000s have brought this issue to the forefront of development economy research (Mohan, 2009). This paper attempts a balanced view of effect of international finance on the developing countries, its benefits and risks involved. To start with, I discuss the needs and benefits of international finance and suggest that with appropriate interventions, developing countries can gain benefits from the long-term positive effects of international finance, though potential risks to the domestic financial sector are more in initial stages of financial globalisation. Then, I describe risks of international finance and the mechanism by which such potential risks lead to financial crises in developing countries triggered by international finance. I review the case of financial crisis of Thailand, to support the viewpoint that rapid exposure of underdeveloped domestic financial sector to international finance is potentially risky (leading to financial crisis) and needs appropriate fiscal and regulatory policy tools to mitigate and overcome financial crisis. Thai financial crisis is an apt case study of how international finance induced twin crises of banking sector and currency (Kaminsky & Reinhart, 1999) in Thailand led to collapse of Thai financial sector, triggering the East Asian financial crisis of 1997–98. The Thai financial crisis reveals some important learning points for the developing countries to deal with international finance. I sum up by observing that developing countries cannot remain isolated and insulated[1] from international finance and financial globalisation, and they should take appropriate measures to gain from benefits of international finance and mitigating its risks, while integrating their domestic financial sector with international financial system. While using the terms 'international finance' and 'financial globalisation' interchangeably in this paper, I dwell on definition proposed by Schmukler (2003), that financial globalisation is a process whereby domestic financial system of a country gets increasingly integrated[2] with international financial markets and institutions. Also, I refer to developing countries as the low and middle income[3] countries, as defined in the World Development Report (The World Bank, 2000).

Why international finance matters for developing countries?

Levine has reviewed the relationship between international finance and domestic long-term economic growth in developing countries and has found 'a strong positive link'. International finance[4] leads to improved resilience of domestic financial system, resulting in increased economic activity and economic growth (Levine, 2005). Developing countries need resources for economic growth, these resources are scarce and need to be invested to produce future resources. This puts a great pressure on developing countries while deciding strategy for utilising available resources for current growth needs vis-à-vis future investment demands. International finance acts to fill this resource gap, thereby easing this pressure (Bowman & Hurry, 1993). As financial globalisation brings in much needed capital in developing economies, it becomes inevitable for these economies to go for international finance (Obstfeld, 2009).

Maximising the benefits from international finance

Since 1990s, there has been a surge in net international finance flow into the developing countries, resulting in substantial current account surplus in these countries (Obstfeld, 2009). Contemporary research has assessed how developing countries benefit from international finance. These benefits accrue in form of consumption smoothing[5] (Zeldes, 1989), availability of capital, strengthening of domestic financial sector, reducing information asymmetries, decrease in adverse selection and moral hazard[6] (Rajan & Zingales, 1998) and attenuation in negative growth – volatility relationship[7] (Kose, Prasad, & Terrones, 2005).

Stulz (2005) argues that existing systemic financial weakness in developing countries severely limits their capacity to gain benefits from international trade and finance. Such weakness may be present in form of imperfect protection of equity investors, unreliable protection of property rights, opaque financial practices and weak rule of law (Stulz, 2005). There is potential risk involved in rapidly exposing underdeveloped domestic financial sector to international finance. According to Schmukler (2003), there is a need to strengthen domestic financial sector and gradually expose it to financial globalisation by using fiscal and policy tools[8] and appropriate supervision and regulatory framework. To ensure and maximise the benefits form international finance, developing countries need to take certain measures. Most of these measures are government led and are directed at deepening domestic financial sector. These measures include adoption of international accounting standards to increase transparency (Schmukler, 2003), improving corporate governance systems so that potential investors can closely monitor corporate management (Stulz, 1999), improvement in technical capabilities of domestic financial institutions for effective operating in precision financing[9] atmosphere of international market (Crockett, 2000), stringent market discipline[10] to regulate macroeconomic, business and financial environment (Stiglitz, 2000), and facilitating entry of foreign banks to bring in the best international banking practices of risk and solvency management[11] (Mishkin, 2003) resulting in domestic banking sector improvement due to competition.

If the abovementioned measures are not taken by the developing countries while engaging with international finance, the institutional weakness would persist. Even if it may not lead to full blown financial crises, this weakness severely limits the gains and benefits of international finance for such countries (Stulz, 2005), emphasising the need of such measures to maximise gains from international finance. Empirical evidence suggests that gains from international finance are maximised when phased implementation of financial globalisation takes place, in the background of strong reserves and external balances position, complemented by growth and stability oriented domestic policies and reforms (Tytell & Wei, 2004).

Risks of international finance

As I have mentioned in my opening remarks, international finance brings with it both the benefits and the risks. To maximise the benefits, developing countries need to take certain measures because their economies have limited capacity to absorb international finance, either due to underdeveloped financial market or due to the fact that they take time to absorb rapid inflow of capital[12] (Prasad, Rajan, Subramanian, Collins, & Henry, 2007). Therefore, a typical requirement of financial globalisation in a developing economy is that the government liberalise domestic financial sector and capital account (Schmukler, 2003).

The measures taken by developing countries to open up their economy to international finance entail various risks in the process, as identified by Obstfeld (2009). These risks are –

a) Undermining of sovereignty due to the contractual terms and conditions imposed by international financing agencies (foreign governments or multilateral agencies);
b) Regulatory arbitrage due to light or no touch regulatory jurisdiction over such international capital, enabling foreign capital to evade domestic supervision;
c) Competitive forbearance whereby domestic financial sector lobbies to weaken domestic regulation pleading parity with international financial intervention;
d) Currency mismatch due to unbalanced position of domestic currency vis-à-vis foreign currency leading to disparity between domestic income and forex liability;
e) Financial contagion as the fear of financial failure may spread from fragile economies to stable economies, affecting them adversely in the process.

These risks may operate independent of each other or concomitantly, and have the potential to disrupt and derail domestic financial sector and economy to result in volatility and crisis (McKinnon & Pill, 1997). If domestic financial system does not have sound fundamentals, and is not covered by prudent regulatory policy, it stands more prone to financial instability caused by such risks (Gourinchas, Valdes, & Landerretche, 2001). Almost all of these risks need government intervention to be tackled, but in the ever-expanding world of financial integration, government is increasingly left with fewer policy instruments,[13] leading to policy challenges of tackling such risks in developing countries (Demirguc-Kunt & Detragiache, 1998). Also, the risks associated with international finance for developing countries are perceived much more if cost of such international capital is high (Calvo, Leiderman, & Reinhart, 1996).

Financial crisis: Causes and mechanism

Financial crisis unfolds due to an interplay of domestic factors and international factors (Obstfeld, 2009). Weak domestic financial fundamentals have been long associated with financial and economic crises induced by foreign capital. But, international finance has inherent imperfections[14] of its own, which might initiate crisis even in countries with sound financial fundamentals (Calvo, Leiderman, & Reinhart, 1996). Financial crisis can happen when foreign investors speculate against domestic currency leading to currency crisis, and eventually to the balance of payment crisis (Diamond & Dybvig, 1983). Similarly, moral hazard can lead to government guarantee backed overborrowing[15] syndrome, substantially augmenting the possibility of financial crisis (McKinnon & Pill, 1997). Financial crisis can also happen when such international finance suddenly pulls out of the country, leading to acute financial distress (Mohan, 2009) even in absence of international imperfections. Similarly, other factors notwithstanding, international financial contagion, which is the financial shock spreading across countries by trade links and financial links,[16] can also lead to crisis in otherwise sound domestic financial sector (Moser, 2003).

Obstfeld (2009) has explained the mechanism of financial crises in developing economies as a multidirectional interaction of four actors[17] – government, banks, currency and corporates. Government and corporates get affected (and then affect each other) by twin crises – banking crisis and currency crisis, leading to financial crisis (Kaminsky & Reinhart, 1999).

I now explain this multidirectional interactive mechanism of financial crisis in a developing economy. Such economy usually faces capital scarcity and therefore, resorts to external forex borrowings. But due to mismatch in borrowing costs and repayment capacity (due to low and volatile tax revenue base), cost of external debt servicing rises, resulting in concomitant devaluation of domestic currency (Krugman, 1979). This puts great pressure on corporates with forex borrowings and domestic banks who advanced loans to such corporates. Such corporates and banks may fail and collapse, so, to prevent this scenario, government bails out such banks, further straining debt servicing. This cycle is repeated till economy slips initially into financial distress, and ultimately into financial crisis. Thus, international finance renders developing economies vulnerable to financial shocks and contagion, triggering financial crisis, though this volatility tends to reduce in the long run with gradual development of domestic financial sector in post financial globalisation period (Schmukler, 2003).

Thailand – the domino of East Asian financial crisis

For almost a decade from 1987–1995, Thai economy was one of the fastest growing economies of the world, growing between 8% to 13% in terms of real GDP and then, Thai financial crisis happened in 1996–1997 (Leightner, 1999), triggering a domino effect for East Asian financial crisis. The Thai financial crisis has been attributed to twin crises – banking crisis and currency crisis, induced by international finance; although banking crisis took the lead, followed by currency crisis (Kaminsky & Reinhart, 1999). Thai financial crisis demonstrates how international finance affects four channels of crisis – government, banks, currency and corporates (Obstfeld, 2009) which interact to trigger and cause financial crisis.

To start with, Thailand had high interest rates coupled with fixed exchange rate. It liberalised its capital account starting from late 1980s, leading to large inflow of international finance as short-term capital (Alba, Hernandez, & Klingebiel, 1999). When real estate bubble burst in 1994, the financial situation of Thai banks and financial companies became precarious due to large exposure to real estate sector. Foreign capital inflows steeply declined and large withdrawals from non-resident Baht accounts (NRBAs) took place, leading to liquidity crunch[18] in banking sector (Montreevat & Rajan, 2001). Bank of Thailand responded by increasing credit supply to banks and financial institutions, but this led to systemic liquidity crisis and erosion of foreign exchange reserves. Devaluation of Thai Baht was a natural corollary of this sequence and Thailand had no other option, but to float its currency (Leightner,

1999). Thai financial crisis formally started in spring 1996 with the collapse of Bangkok Bank of Commerce due to mounting non-performing real estate loans,[19] progressed in March 1997, when Thai government suspended the stock trading[20] for all banking and finance companies, and culminated in July 1997 with floating of Baht by the Bank of Thailand (Leightner & Knox Lovell, 1998). To overcome this crisis, Thai government launched a massive financial sector restructuring and strengthening program in 1997, which included nationalising, merging and closing down certain financial institutions, recapitalisation of banks and entry of foreign banks into Thailand.

Learnings and the Way Forward

There are important lessons to be learnt from Thai financial crisis. These learning points are in the form of measures which developing countries need to take to gain benefits from international finance and to minimise its entailing risks. Most of these steps are government led, and the notion that market can remedy the weakness has been found to be incorrect (Mohan, 2009). First and most important lesson is that, the exposure to international finance in form of financial globalisation must be gradual and cautious (Demirguc-Kunt & Detragiache, 1998), and while doing so, the domestic financial sector must have strong fundamentals with well-placed supervision and regulation, and the overall macroeconomic environment should be stable (Montreevat & Rajan, 2001). It is generally agreed that domestic financial sector cannot remain insulated and isolated from the forces of financial globalisation and ever increasing global financial integration. Empirical research indicates that international finance is beneficial for the developing countries in the long run, its risks gradually subside as the domestic financial system gradually develops and deepens to deal with it. As the reasons of international finance induced financial crisis are more domestic than international (Schmukler, 2003), the developing countries should ideally respond to it by correcting domestic imperfections of banking, currency and regulation.

Conclusion

International finance brings in profound benefits for developing economies, but entails grave risks too. Developing countries can maximise gain from its benefits and mitigate its risks by taking certain measures while engaging with it. In this paper, I give a context of why international finance matters for developing countries. Then I underline its benefits and discuss how developing countries can gain from these benefits by taking certain measures. Subsequently, I highlight the risks of international finance these measures entail and discuss the causes of these risks. Then I focus on the financial crisis, its risks and causes, and mechanism of how it is triggered by international finance. While discussing the case of Thai financial crisis, I trace how and why this crisis unfolded in 1990s, and the measures taken by Thai government to recover from it. Ultimately, drawing from the lessons from Thai financial crisis, I support my argument that sudden and rapid exposure of underdeveloped and unprepared domestic financial sector to international finance is highly risky and certain measures need to be taken by developing countries to mitigate these risks and gain from benefits of international finance by a careful and gradual exposure to it. To be positively adaptive to international finance, developing countries need to incorporate three core components in their economy – market led exchange rate, gradual opening of capital account and sound monetary policy framework ensuring price stabilisation (The World Bank, 2006). As increasing financial integration is a reality in the ever-expanding globalisation process, there is an inevitability for the developing countries to face increasing exposure to international finance, however, also substantially increasing the scope for them to benefit from such exposure in their economic development.

Notes

1. As cross-country trade is a necessity, the concept of financial insulation is, at best, hypothetical (Krugman, 1979).

2. Financial integration essentially involves liberalisation of domestic financial sector and capital account. It leads to liberal cross-country movement of international capital with active participation of domestic borrowers and international lenders, through international financial intermediaries (Schmukler, 2003).

3. Emerging markets are essentially middle-income economies (The World Bank, 2000).

4. Levine had included both the availability of international finance and functioning of domestic financial system in his work, for more details, refer to Levine (2005).

5. Consumption smoothing implies that consumers desire stable and predictable consumption, and they might sacrifice some consumption in the present to have a stable consumption in the long-term future (Zeldes, 1989).

6. Adverse selection means that 'low-quality borrowers' seek out capital in the market, leading to credit rationing, eventually pushing the interest rates upwards. Moral hazard means that

borrowers use the capital in certain risky ways, not beneficial to the lenders.

7. Countries which are more liberal to international finance and trade experience less severe trade-off between economic growth and systemic financial volatility (Kose, Prasad, & Terrones, 2005).

8. Schmukler has identified such tools as counter cyclical fiscal policy, price stabilisation mechanism, active forex reserve management, contingent liquidity provisioning, prudential regulation and increased market discipline based on reducing incomplete information and information asymmetries.

9. According to Crockett (2000), precision finance involves unbundling, repackaging, pricing and redistributing financial risks with the assistance of information and communication technology.

10. This includes having controls on inflow and outflow of short-term capital while attracting international finance. Stiglitz (2000) suggests these measures to minimise the gap between social and private costs and to stabilise short-term international capital shifts.

11. Foreign banks bring in more diversified portfolio, better risk management practices and better handling of solvency with them and domestic banks have to adopt these practices to hold on to their business in competitive banking (Mishkin, 2003).

12. In developing economies, rapid inflow of foreign capital fuels rapid consumption growth, and these economies take time to absorb the impact of this (Prasad, Rajan, Subramanian, Collins, & Henry, 2007).

13. As the government is supposed to open up the economy more and more, it is expected to let go its controls and interventions in favour of market led interventions.

14. These imperfections manifest in the form of bubble generation, irrational investing behaviour, herding tendencies, speculative attacks on domestic currency and market crashes (Calvo, Leiderman, & Reinhart, 1996).

15. According to McKinnon and Pill (1997), when such domestic borrowers fail to service these loans, international

lenders invoke sovereign guarantee on such borrowings, plunging the government into financial crisis.

16. Moser (2003) explains that when there are trade and financial links between two countries, currency devaluation in first country adversely affects competitive advantage of the second, leading to deliberate devaluation of currency by the second country to rebalance the scenario.

17. Obstfled (2009) refers to these actors as channels of crises.

18. Between January 1996 and June 1997, capital outflow form NRBAs was to the tune of US $8.2 billion.

19. When it collapsed in 1996 spring, the Bangkok Bank of Commerce had total NPAs amounting to nearly half of its total assets, at US $3.5 billion, almost all of these were the real estate loans.

20. When the stock trading was suspended in Thailand for banking and finance companies on March 3, 1997, it was for the first time since 1976, that this kind of action was taken by the government.

IV

INDIA'S TRYST WITH GST

An Unparalleled PFM Reform

With the stroke of 12 O'clock midnight on 30th June 2016, India embarked on an ambitious journey of the biggest tax reform since independence, by rolling out the Goods and Services Tax (GST). The literature is replete with success of Indian GST as a phenomenal indirect tax reform and a PFM reform, unparalleled in the history of global economy, but there is scant discussion on the challenges that GST as a PFM reform has imparted for fiscal federalism in India. This paper attempts to fill this gap by highlighting these challenges. I start with contextual and conceptual discussion on GST as a PFM reform in the peculiar economic and political environment of India. Then I elaborate how GST as a unique experiment in Indian fiscal federalism has started a new chapter in cooperative fiscal federalism and strengthened it by way of the GST Council (GSTC) and GST Network (GSTN). Following this, I identify and briefly describe important challenges presented by GST for Indian fiscal federalism and the implications of these challenges. I argue that GST is a success story in indirect tax reforms, and the challenges to fiscal federalism are not due to GST per se, but due to the peculiar design and administration of GST. I conclude by stating that though the challenges created by GST for fiscal federalism in India would continue till the states start perceiving a fair fiscal treatment and trust in their fiscal relationship with the centre, yet it would be far-fetched to say that GST may fail as a PFM reform due to these challenges. For purpose of this paper, I use the term 'centre' and 'central government' interchangeably to refer to Government of India; and the term 'states' and 'state governments' interchangeably to refer collectively to Governments of 28 Indian States and 3 Union Territories with legislature.

The context and concept

Public financial management (PFM) relates to revenue portion and spending portion of the government, in turn affecting allocation of resources and distribution of income (Harvey & Gayer, 2008, p. 16). Revenue portion concerns the taxation and spending portion primarily concerns the budget – the two key elements of PFM (Wescott, 2008). Historical debate on fiscal federalism and fiscal decentralisation revolves around the problem of revenue assignment (Bahl & Martinez-Vazquez, 2006). Revenue assignment problem has two aspects – which level of government should be assigned which taxes and, what functions and decision-making authority should be devolved at which level (Mascagni, 2016). Expenditure assignment, which means which level of government spends how much in managing its services, is an important aspect of revenue assignment (Bird, 2012). Other widely accepted principles of revenue assignment include adequacy, buoyancy, stability, efficiency, equity, autonomy, administrative and political feasibility and consistency (Smoke, 2013). To prevent economic and distribution distortions and regional imbalances, it is essential to decide revenue assignment based on expenditure assignment and these principles (Mascagni, 2016). Only then, it would be possible to achieve true fiscal decentralisation in a federal structure rather than just delegation or deconcentration (Bahl & Martinez-Vazquez, 2006).

In this paper, I focus on the Goods and Services Tax (GST), the most recent PFM reform of India and hailed as the biggest indirect taxation reform in the PFM history of India so far (Government of India, 2017). GST is a comprehensive, uniform, destination-based, multi-stage, value added consumption tax on goods and services in India launched since July 2017 (Mukherjee, 2019). In GST regime, every stage of value addition attracts Central GST (CGST), State GST (SGST), as well as Integrated GST (IGST) for inter-state transactions, in the process reducing tax cascading, transaction costs and improving tax compliance (Government of India, 2017). GST regime has an inbuilt 5-year compensation period (from July 2017 to June 2022), wherein states' SGST revenues are protected by central compensation to the extent of such SGST shortfall from projected 14% growth. The idea of GST was conceived in 2006 by the Kelkar Task Force on Fiscal Responsibility and Budget Management Act, 2003. It took over a decade of deliberations for the centre and the states to come to a consensus and pass the GST Act in Parliament and State Legislatures in 2017 (GST Council, 2020). These deliberations centred around the problem of revenue assignment – who will tax what and how, and laid down the design and operation of GST. The GST is a reform on revenue portion side of PFM in India and concerns the taxation, specifically the indirect taxation. GST, by design, has led to the centre sharing its tax base with states (arising from excise duty, service tax and part of custom duty). In return, GST gives centre powers to tax the tax base of states (arising from sales tax, VAT, central sales tax, entry tax, luxury tax, entertainment tax, purchase tax and tax on lottery, betting and gambling) (Mukherjee & Rao, 2019). As the GST has rearranged and reassigned the indirect taxes between the central and state governments, it is essentially an exercise in the revenue assignment.

In India, the 3-tier intergovernmental relations involve centre, states and local governments. Traditionally, central governments have exerted more control over revenue generation, collection and distribution (Smoke, 2013), and this is the case in India too. GST, which was conceived to be an indirect tax reform, has eventually materialised as a revenue sharing mechanism governed by a pre-set formula for intergovernmental transfer. Such transfer is seen more as an "unearned" revenue source than an "earned" taxation base (Mascagni, 2016). Unearned because, the states are not earning tax from revenue sources from which they earned such taxes pre-GST, due to GST subsuming such taxes.

India is a union of states (and union territories). Presently the central government and state governments are formed by as many as 14 political parties and as many coalitions of varying ideology and composition (The Commonwealth Secretariat, 2020). Further, as a developing economy with a narrow taxation base, the tax kitty of the country usually misses the budgetary targets year after year, making sufficient fiscal devolution of this kitty a difficult exercise between various levels of government, often laced with an atmosphere of fiscal mistrust between the states and the central government (Chakraborty, 2019). Maintaining healthy and engaging fiscal relations in this particular economic and political environment is a major issue for the policy makers and stakeholders. GST as a PFM reform has positively influenced and affected the Indian fiscal federalism as I would discuss now.

GST and Indian fiscal federalism

GST is a unique experiment in fiscal federalism in India. Indian model of cooperative fiscal federalism is characterised by well-defined taxation rights, expenditure responsibilities and inter-governmental fiscal transfer system, tackling both the vertical and horizontal imbalances[1] (Kelkar, 2019). As GST provides a dual VAT (Value Added Tax) format with concurrent taxation powers to both central and state governments, it has influenced fiscal federalism in India both horizontally and vertically (Mukherjee, 2019). Horizontally means among the states, as GST marks a shift from production-based taxation to destination-based taxation, leading to gains for states with larger consumption base vis-à-vis those with larger production base. Vertically means between the centre and states, as GST revenue sharing happens by intergovernmental fiscal transfer from centre to states. A gamechanger in the saga of India's fiscal federalism, GST has united a country of 1.3 billion people into a common market by dismantling inter-state tariff barriers once for all, to usher in the proverbial 'one nation, one tax, one market' in India (GST Council, 2020). GST has been instrumental in achieving harmonisation of tax rules and regulations, procedures and processes, compliance and tax base across the central and state governments to achieve its ambition of improving ease-of-doing business in India (Agrawal, Basu, Ghosh, Pareek, & Zhang, 2019). With the launching of GST, India has embarked on a new fiscal federalism, with GST as one of the three pillars.[2]

GST Council (GSTC) – furthering fiscal federalism

I would now discuss the elements that determine success of GST as a PFM reform in India. Beginning with France in 1954, GST/ VAT has been implemented in more than 160 countries in the world so far, but what differentiates the Indian GST regime from other countries is the GST Council (GSTC) (Central Board of Indirect Taxes and Customs, 2019). GSTC has been created by 101st Constitutional Amendment in 2016, to oversee implementation of GST and to recommend on GST rates, exemption and thresholds, taxes to be subsumed and other related matters (Government of India, 2017). GSTC is unique to India without any parallels in the world. No other country has a similar constitutional body, representative of both the national and sub-national provincial governments to collectively decide the fiscal principles of tax revenue distribution, as the GSTC in India (Chakraborty, 2019). Creation of GSTC to implement a commonly agreed GST agenda is a landmark event in history of India's fiscal federalism (Kelkar, 2019), a new chapter in history of India's centre-states relations, with full fiscal decision-making powers and control over fiscal health of the country (Government of India, 2017).

GSTC as the mechanism to implement GST has resulted in a fundamental change in Indian fiscal federalism and is the actual third pillar of federalism as suggested by Kelkar (2019). GSTC has emerged as an open platform for the states in India to meaningfully engage in fiscal deliberations and negotiations with the central government, as active participants in fiscal decision-making process, which is the essence of Indian cooperative federalism (Chakraborty, 2019). This is evident by the fact that in 39 meetings of GSTC held till date, all decisions have been based on consensus-building deliberations between the centre and states without any need of voting (GST Council, 2020). Whereas previously centre and states were merely 'good fiscal neighbours', GSTC has transformed them as 'equal fiscal partners' sharing a common indirect tax base (Kelkar, 2019).

The information technology backbone for the GST has been provided by the Goods and Services Network (GSTN) by creating a one-stop GST portal for all stakeholders – traders-taxpayers, tax authorities, banks and governments (Government of India, 2017). All returns are filed, tax paid and refunds happen on the GST portal only. Further, there is a single return system on the GSTN in place of old system of multiple returns, facilitating the need of reconciliation of tax liability arising at every level. The GSTN is one of the tools of the GST regime to strengthen the fiscal federalism because this system makes sure that information on amount of due Input Tax Credit (ITC) to the states from the centre is available online in real-time for the states and central government. When the states receive their share based on GSTN data, they are reassured that they are getting their due from the central government, in a manner which is transparent and beyond doubt (Agrawal, Basu, Ghosh, Pareek, & Zhang, 2019), addressing the major irritant of fiscal mistrust in centre-states relations. GSTC, along with GSTN have emerged as the main elements which have ensured the success of GST in boosting the cooperative fiscal federalism in India.

GST Challenges for Indian fiscal federalism and their implications

Though GST has been labelled as a successful indirect tax reform in India, I would now discuss the elements that act as challenges of GST for fiscal federalism as a PFM reform. These challenges do not stem out of the GST per se, but due to peculiar mechanism in which GST has been designed and is being administered. As I have mentioned earlier, the issue of revenue assignment and sharing of "unearned" revenue source rather than an "earned" taxation base (Mascagni, 2016) lies in the background of these challenges.

Implementing a tax reform as big and ambitious as the GST in a diverse and federal setting as in India impinges on reconciliation of states' fiscal interests with those of the centre. As GST regime safeguards the SGST shortfall for 5 years in form of central compensation to the states, it is necessary to calculate such compensation component by comparing revenue fluctuation arising post-GST, with pre-GST revenues. But, disaggregated pre-GST revenue data is not available either in Union Budget documents or States' Finance Accounts for those items which are now under GST and for those still out of GST (Mukherjee, 2019). Thus, it is difficult to estimate revenue loss due to out-of-GST items. This may not financially affect the states presently, but when central compensation ceases in 2022, SGST shortfall would have to be absorbed solely by the states. To avoid this, states would lobby to extend GST compensation beyond 2022, but accommodating this demand may not be fiscally prudent for central government. In that scenario, states may assert in GSTC to set their own SGST rates in tune with their fiscal situation, leading to GST rate wars among states, and disrupting the harmonised GST (Mukherjee, 2019). This may lead to a voting in the GSTC meetings, which would favour the central government due to the fact that Centre has a weightage of one-third of total votes cast, while the states have a two-third weightage (GST Council, 2020). This relatively less bargaining power of states in GSTC renders states to a disadvantageous position vis-a-vis the centre (Reddy, 2019), which does not augur well for the spirit of cooperative fiscal federalism in India. In the Exploratory Notes for State Formats, 13th Finance Commission has observed that pervasive feeling in the states is that their fiscal autonomy and flexibility would be compromised post-GST, more so in case of states with larger manufacturing base, as GST will permanently dent their revenues in favour of states with larger consumption base (Jha, 2013). Thus, GST has not been perceived by the states to strengthen cooperative fiscal federalism to the extent it was expected to, due to its very design (Ranade, 2019). The 'grand bargain' of GST in its present form is seen as an asymmetric bargain for the states in fiscal autonomy (Kelkar, 2019).

Secondly, in GST regime, centre administers CGST and IGST; and states administer SGST. But entire IGST collection is not available to centre as tax revenue, because Input Tax Credit (ITC) remains in transition till another GST liability (CGST, SGST or IGST) arises in downstream of value chain in form of credit invoice. This means that centre needs to settle ITC claims of states without actually realising IGST, from CGST kitty, at the cost of central revenues (Mukherjee, 2019). This has created a serious fiscal stress for the centre in fiscal devolution exercise.

Thirdly, in India, principles governing the intergovernmental fiscal transfers are recommended by Finance Commission (FC), a constitutional body, based on projected expenditure and revenue collection. Post-GST, another constitutional body has come into existence in form of the GSTC. Co-existence of two constitutional bodies with concurrent jurisdiction on intergovernmental fiscal transfers has created overlapping grey areas on the ways to monitor, scrutinise and optimise revenue outcomes (Drabu, 2019).

Though, it is essential to have a well-defined coordination mechanism between FC and GSTC, yet such a mechanism is conspicuous by its absence. The overlap in functioning of the FC and GSTC is likely to adversely impact uniformity of recommendations on likely revenue of states, sustainable growth rates and revenue deficits for consideration of central grants to states (Singh, 2019). There is an imminent need to develop an institutional relationship mechanism between the GSTC and FC to achieve coordination and conflict resolution (Drabu, 2019).

Indian experience so far has showed that GST as the third pillar of New Fiscal Federalism is still evolving (Kelkar, 2019) and needs to quickly tackle these challenges. GST, as a standalone indirect tax reform, is a phenomenal success. But, as a PFM reform, it would need to overcome the challenges posed to fiscal federalism, until the states start perceiving fair fiscal treatment and develop trust in their fiscal relationship with the centre, in true spirit of cooperative fiscal federalism (Ranade, 2019). These challenges, if not addressed timely and adequately, have the potential to outweigh the benefits of GST and cooperative fiscal federalism ushered by GST, by a phenomenon of competitive fiscal federalism in India (Das, 2019). Though it would be too far-fetched to say that these challenges may lead to failure of GST as a PFM reform in India (Ranade, 2019).

Conclusion

GST is not merely a success saga in the indirect taxation system overhaul of unprecedented magnitude transforming India as an economic union, but also has impacted fiscal federalism considerably all along, commencing new fiscal federalism. In this paper, I have attempted to highlight these impacts and challenges of GST for India's fiscal federalism. I have started by setting the context and elaborating the concept of GST as a PFM reform in peculiar economic and political environment of India. I have pointed out how GST has affected and strengthened fiscal federalism by way of GSTC and GSTN mechanism. I have identified and analysed important challenges that have arisen for Indian fiscal federalism as India moves forward with GST. I have suggested that GST, in its present form, is still an evolving pillar of India's fiscal federalism, as the states are yet to perceive the element of fiscal trust and fairness in the GST regime; yet, it would be far-fetched to say that GST may fail as a PFM reform due to these challenges. I have inferred that elements of success of GST as a PFM reform in India flow from the fiscal trust of the states on centre, translating into reality through the use of technology (GSTN) and participatory decision making involving both levels of government (GSTC) in particular Indian economic and political environment. While the final outcome of GST on fiscal federalism in India would be known in the coming years when the states beginning to play out in the domain of realpolitik, it is important that GST keeps evolving to meet up such challenges and aspirations of states as is required in true spirit of cooperative fiscal federalism.

Notes

1. Vertical imbalance arises when different levels of government – central, state and local governments in Indian context, have asymmetric taxation powers vis-à-vis their expenditure responsibilities in the scheme of fiscal federalism. Horizontal

imbalance arises when different government authorities prescribe differential tax rates within their jurisdiction for providing public goods of comparable quantity and quality, e.g., different city governments levy different rates of water tax in India. For more information, see Kelkar (2019).

2. Kelkar (2019) identifies three main pillars of New Fiscal Federalism in India – Finance Commission, NITI Ayog and now GST.

V

GOVERNMENT AS A DEVELOPMENT ACTOR

GeM and Inclusive Business for Indian MSEs

The concept of inclusive business, led by inclusive markets approach of UNDP, focuses on how private sector can contribute to reduction of poverty to help achieve Millennium Development Goals (MDGs). It has often been argued that under right market conditions, private sector can alleviate poverty by generating jobs and income for the poor. UNDP also factors in the role of a strong and effective state for the private sector to usher in development for low-income communities. But, most of the discussion on inclusive business revolves around the role of private sector, or the business itself, as a development actor. This paper attempts to provide an alternative view, focusing on the role of other major stakeholder in development – the government, as a development actor in contributing to poverty alleviation and achievement of development objectives. The private sector does not do business with private entities only, governments are also big buyers for businesses. A developing economy like India spends a fifth of its annual GDP on public procurement, an indication of how much business the government does with the businesses. Thus, government, as a big buyer, plays an important role in creating and sustaining business chains in the economy, fulfilling its role as a development actor. To support this alternative view, I refer to the case of Government e-Marketplace (GeM), an end-to-end e-commerce platform developed by Government of India for public procurement. GeM shows how government has helped poor producers and small businesses, which I collectively refer to as the micro and small enterprises (MSEs) in this paper, to develop their knowledge and skills, infrastructure, and a level playing legal-regulatory framework, enabling them to participate in business opportunities. In next section, I discuss UNDP constraints-strategies matrix for inclusive business as the conceptual framework for this paper. The UNDP matrix is the best fit to explain my case as it deals with constraints the MSEs face in developing economies and strategies provided by inclusive business approach of government to overcome some of these. Further, I explain the concepts of inclusive business, government as a development actor and micro and small enterprises (MSEs), as defined by Government of India Act of 2006, in context of this paper. Next, I highlight the Government e-Marketplace (GeM), its background, salient features, and how it has helped MSEs in India achieve inclusivity in business, by referring to statistics from GeM dashboard. In next section, I analyse in detail the UNDP matrix of inclusive business strategies and market constraints for small businesses like MSEs to show how Government e-Marketplace (GeM) is promoting inclusive business for MSEs in India. I sum up by mentioning that, though GeM has not able to remove all constraints to inclusive business for MSEs, yet it has successfully addressed some of these constraints by adopting inclusion strategies identified by the UNDP, to achieve inclusivity for such MSEs in business in India and furthering the role of government as a development actor in promoting inclusive business for these MSEs.

Discussion of key concepts

UNDP framework to understand role of government as enabler of inclusive business

The GeM is a case of 'do more' approach (McFalls, 2017) and 'do better or do more good' approach (Sayer, 2006) to achieve inclusive business outcomes. The 'do more' approach deals with doing more business by tapping untapped business opportunities, whereas 'do better or do more good' approach deals with interventions to make business more profitable and less risky. GeM is a platform to work "through" the state to achieve deep marketisation in developing economy like India. The right regulatory environment enables growth by providing enabling environment to facilitate private sector activity (Carroll, 2012), and GeM has helped in creating that right and enabling environment for such MSEs. As the GeM handbook mentions, and I quote,

> *"GeM shall promote inclusiveness, which means that all Government buyers and sellers shall be accepted on the platform. GeM shall aspire to create a robust seller base and all sellers interested in conducting business with the Government shall be welcomed on the platform. For buyers and sellers that do not have the know-how of using GeM, additional assistance in the form of focused training, onboarding sessions and continued feedback and support shall be provided."*

Of these different approaches to explain role of government in inclusive business, in this paper, I employ the UNDP matrix of inclusive business strategies and market constraints for small businesses like MSEs, as the conceptual framework, to show how GeM is promoting inclusive business for MSEs in India. UNDP matrix, as shown in Figure 5.1 below, is the best fit to explain my case here as it deals with constraints faced by MSEs in developing economies and strategies provided by inclusive business approach to these MSEs to overcome some of these constraints. The GeM is an example of how the government can also use some of these strategies to promote inclusive business just like the businesses do, which I shall explore later in this chapter.

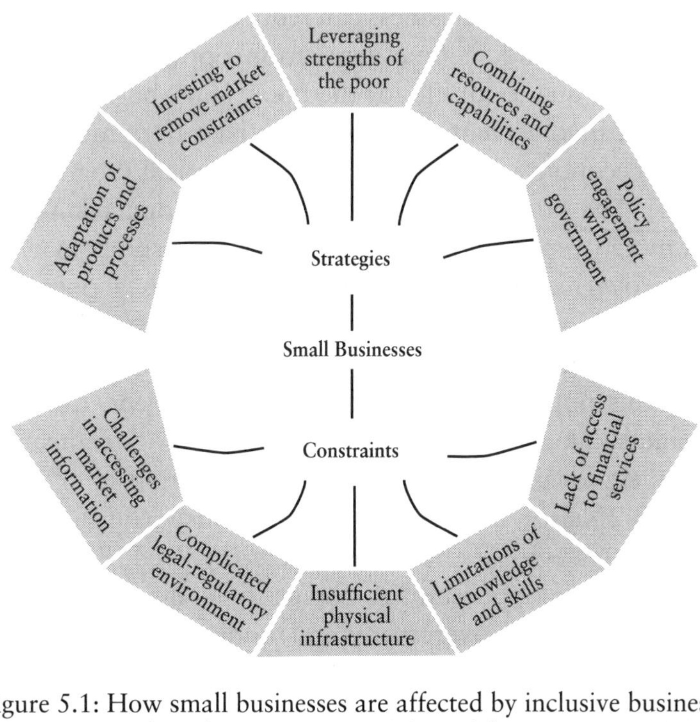

Figure 5.1: How small businesses are affected by inclusive business strategies and market constraints (Adapted from UNDP, 2008)

Inclusive business

The inclusive business approach tries to overcome socio-economic challenges by including poor communities in business chains (Likoko & Kini, 2017) and by generating opportunities for a decent and sustainable income generation for such communities having no or low mobility in job market (Teodosio & Comini, 2012). When included in business chain, such low income population and small producers provide market and workforce to strengthen business supply chains (United Nations Development Programme, 2010). Business can reduce poverty by creating employment and income generation opportunities, thus improving quality of life for the poor. Thus, business leads to direct involvement of those at the base of pyramid into market economy (United Nations Development Programme, 2004). The poorest two-third of world's population does not merely represent a massive untapped consumer market, the proverbial base of pyramid, but also is a potential major source of manpower, producers and suppliers for big companies in emerging markets. Business can engage with this population by providing employment, training, business linkages, market access and technology transfer in the quest for income generation and reduction of extreme poverty (Nelson & Prescott, 2008). Inclusive business is a win-all strategy for the stakeholders involved. Businesses gain by new opportunities for growth, innovation and competitiveness. Governments and funding agencies gain by having a self-sustaining and self-multiplying development impact with minimum or no funding requirement. The poor gain by getting greater access, choice and opportunity for them in life and livelihood (Jenkins & Ishikawa, 2010). McFalls has compared corporate philanthropic ventures and commercial ventures and suggested that inclusive business tends to maximise both social and economic benefits for low-income communities. For a not-for-profit corporate philanthropic venture, the social benefits as well as the economic benefits remain low. In such a scenario, when there is an effort to maximise the social benefits, such efforts do not sustain in long run due to low economic benefits. Conversely, any conscious effort to maximise economic benefits also is not sustainable because the social benefits of serving the community is adversely affected. Same is true in case of pure commercial ventures, which have only economic profitability motto, and do not concern with social benefits of such profits. Inclusive business, with its focus on local community involvement and localized profit motive, is able to maximise both the social and economic benefits for such low-income communities (McFalls, 2017, p. 142).

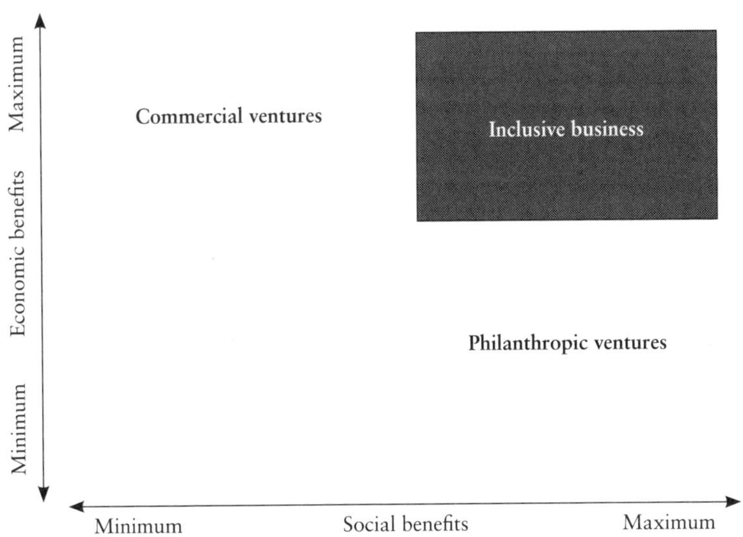

Figure 5.2: Maximisation of economic and social benefits by inclusive business (Adapted from McFalls 2017, p. 142).

Government as a development actor: An alternative approach to inclusive business

As I have discussed above, traditional approach to inclusive business and its role in development pivots around business as a development actor. This paper attempts to take an alternative to this approach by highlighting the role of government as a development actor in achieving inclusive business. Government is also a big buyer in the market by way of large public procurements, thus it is not only the businesses which add to market activity. For instance, about 20% of India's GDP is spent on public procurement annually (Lal, 2018). Role of government as a development actor becomes critical in developing economies. The solution to poverty lies in developing "large-scale and wide-spread" entrepreneurship. It is the collaboration of government with civil society, poor and businesses which can result in fast growing markets at the bottom of pyramid to eradicate poverty (Prahalad, 2005, p. 4). Such entrepreneurial solutions have minimal or no financial burden on government in developing countries. The enabling atmosphere provided by government for innovative entrepreneurship helps reduce poverty by creating opportunities for the poor (Prahalad, 2005, p. 5). Firms seeking to adopt inclusive business strategies for low-income producers and consumers face systemic limitations in the form of lack of infrastructure, low skills and knowledge levels and limited access to cheaper finance.

It is for these issues that the government needs to step in and address them, enabling business to achieve optimum inclusivity (Jenkins & Ishikawa, 2010). Pure market-based poverty reduction approaches have not been sufficiently effective, therefore, role of government is critical to create an enabling atmosphere to facilitate inclusive business (Ashley, 2009). It is the responsibility of government to provide right environment, thereby enabling business to deliver and enabling poor to participate. Thus, government plays development actor by setting a context in which business achieves optimum development outcomes (United Nations Development Programme, 2008). Inclusive business needs a supportive environment to tackle the market challenges of low-income communities. This is provided by government in form of information, investment, incentive and implementation support in terms of encouraging entrepreneurship and building capacities of small businesses (United Nations Development Programme, 2013).

Micro and small enterprises (MSEs) and their importance in inclusive business

In this paper, I have used the terms "micro enterprises" and "small enterprises", as defined in the Micro, Small and Medium Enterprises Development Act, 2006, of Government of India. This Act defines micro and small

Table 5.1: Definition of micro and small enterprises (Government of India, 2019).

Type	Manufacturing enterprises	Service enterprises
Micro enterprises	Investment in plant and machinery not exceeding INR 2.5 million	Investment in equipment not exceeding INR 1 million
Small enterprises	Investment in plant and machinery more than INR 2.5 million but not exceeding INR 50 million	Investment in equipment more than INR 1 million but not exceeding INR 20 million

enterprises in terms of investment in plant and machinery for the manufacturing enterprises, and in terms of investment in equipment for the service enterprises (Government of India, 2019) as shown in Table 5.1.

Inclusive business approach can have varied positive influences on development outcomes, but such influence and impact are significant for development of micro and small enterprises (MSEs). MSEs constitute a critical component of inclusive business strategy and are crucial to its success in developing economies. Going by the definition, it becomes clear that MSEs operate at the lowest level of business hierarchy, mostly informally, in the lowest section of low-income population. MSEs constitute the bulk of micro, small and medium enterprises (MSMEs) in developing countries. They drive local entrepreneurship, production, innovation and employment to act as the backbone of economic activity. Such MSEs involve local community in which they operate, as workforce and consumers, as they better understand local needs and aspirations. However, in developing countries, MSEs have to face an unfavourable environment in terms of lack of knowledge and skills, poor infrastructure and difficult or no access to cheaper finance, adversely affecting their capabilities and potential to contribute to development goals (McFalls, 2017, p. 142). There is a widespread lack of motivation, low income, poor or no reinvestment, lack of market access and support networks ailing the small businesses in developing countries, a phenomenon labelled as 'survival entrepreneurship' (Vossenberg, 2016). In this scenario, large businesses can use inclusive business approach to build business linkages with these MSEs to significantly improve the situation of such enterprises and take them out of this survival entrepreneurship.

GOVERNMENT E-MARKETPLACE (GEM)

I use the Government e-Marketplace as a case study to explain how government is promoting inclusive business for the micro and small enterprises (MSEs) in India. GeM is an apt case as it shows how government as development actor has helped MSEs overcome some of the constraints faced by them, by providing an enabling atmosphere for them, and to include them in large government procurement process as suppliers of goods and services.

India's nominal GDP at current prices in 2019 has been projected at around USD 3 trillion, making it the 5th largest economy in the world (IMF World Economic Outlook, 2019). An estimated 20% of India's GDP is spent on public procurement annually (Lal, 2018), the amount was USD 340 billion in financial year 2018–2019 and is likely to keep pace as India looks to achieve a USD 5 trillion economy by 2025 (Centre for Public Impact, 2019). This government purchase has not been without challenges. Multitudes of purchases in smaller quantities made independently by various ministries, departments and public sector units of the government have been vulnerable to inconsistencies in public procurement processes on one hand, and opaque transactions emanating from buyer-supplier interaction on the other. Micro and small enterprises (MSEs) found it almost impossible to reach the buyers in government setup due to multiple and complicated procedural layers, which substantially pushed up their cost and rendered them uncompetitive in government purchase procedures. To deal with the challenge, Government of India launched GeM, an e-commerce platform in August 2016. GeM is an end-to-end marketplace reform in the form of a private consortium comprising of an e-commerce player, a systems integrator and an IT infrastructure provider, which operates under the GeM Special Purpose Vehicle (GeMSPV) of Government of India. The platform is presumed to have led to savings of up to 25% in government expenditure while enhancing transparency and efficiency in public procurement (Centre for Public Impact, 2019). At full scale of operations, savings from GeM will have a significant impact on lowering fiscal deficit of the country.

GeM is a fully online and transparent platform with a mandate that all government procurement of products and services has to be from the GeM, unless such items are not available on GeM. Like any other e-commerce platform, GeM hosts a listing of products and services divided under various categories, wherein buyers can search, compare and buy products online. GeM ensures that any entrepreneur can list products to sell directly to the government, avoiding red-tape and corruption. This has enabled many MSEs to participate in the formal business of government procurement. The MSEs can start selling to government from anywhere in India. In a short time span of less than 4 years since its launch, GeM has witnessed transactions over USD 5.8 billion, involving sales

Table 5.2: GeM statistics as on 01-01-2020
(The GeM dashboard, Government of India)

Transaction value INR 40,432 cr (USD 6.08 B)	Orders handled so far 28,55,597	Sellers and service providers listed 3,24,619
Products listed 15,60,076 (in 393 major and 1,053 minor product categories)	Services listed 20,619 (in 13 service categories)	Buyer organisations 40,960
MSE sellers of total sellers 62,085	Order value percentage of MSEs of total orders 50.74	Total current e-tenders listed 1,00,000

of over 1.5 million products and services from over 324,000 sellers, including over 62,000 MSEs. Government of India has set an ambitious business target of USD 75 billion on GeM platform within 5 years of its launch, by the end of financial year 2021–2022 (Government of India, 2019). These figures are shown in Table 5.2.

GeM interventions to promote inclusive business as per the UNDP framework

I now explain the constraints faced by MSEs in India and how GeM has helped overcome some of these by adopting strategies to integrating these MSEs as suppliers into sustainable business chain as local supply partners (McFalls, 2017, p. 143). For this purpose, I employ the UNDP constraints-strategies inclusive business framework as discussed earlier, to underline the constraints and the strategies used by government to tackle some of these.

Market information

As has been identified by the UNDP, small businesses have no market information available to them as to the preferences and demands of consumers and as to the products and services they need to offer as businesses (United Nations Development Programme, 2008). In Indian context, prior to GeM coming into being, there was a lack of market information for MSEs regarding demand, prices, and also processes to meet this demand. Market was controlled by a handful of suppliers who could seek government approvals as suppliers and vendors by a tortuous and opaque process, rendering the government procurement system vulnerable to monopoly and cartelization. The rate contracts, so finalized, were valid for a limited period varying from 1 year to 3 years, necessitating the repetition of entire process periodically. This resulted in MSEs getting limited access to government procurement.

In tune with the UNDP "adopt products and processes" strategy, GeM has been a game changer for some of these constraints to accessing market information by MSEs. GeM has shown how government can work around market constraints by adopting strategies using information technology to create inclusivity for MSEs in economy. All purchases more than INR 5,00,000 need to be made by open electronic bidding process on GeM website, which is accessible to all registered MSEs on GeM portal to participate in. This process, being paperless and contactless, enables any MSE to participate in the e-tender process.

Government has also gained from what UNDP has labelled as "leverage the strengths of the poor" strategy, with a reported 27% saving in procurement cost on GeM portal (The Economic Times, 2019). It is because MSEs are able to quote competitive prices for their products and services on GeM platform due to their lower overheads, leading to a win-win situation for both government buyers and MSE sellers.

Regulatory environment

UNDP has identified ineffective regulatory environment as a constraint for small businesses to work. This effectively means that small businesses like MSEs lack protection and opportunities provided by a well-functioning legal-regulatory system. In Indian context, this may be understood by the fact that prior to GeM coming into being, it was a tedious and lengthy process for the MSEs to get registered as suppliers with government departments due to voluminous paper work, and taking up to 3 months or more for the registration process to complete (The Economic Times, 2019). Similarly, MSEs and startups would not qualify for government orders as they had no pre-requisite supply experience to produce while registering.

GeM demonstrates the UNDP strategy of "invest in removing market constraints" to achieve an enabling regulatory environment for MSEs. Government of India invested INR 200 crore (USD 30 M) in GeMSPV (GeM Special Purpose Vehicle) to develop and launch GeM by replacing the archaic Directorate General of Supplies and Disposals (DGS&D) system to usher in an inclusive system of doing business with government for the MSEs (GeM handbook, Government of India, 2019). GeM has done away with supply experience as a pre-requisite qualification for MSEs to participate in government buying, opening the flood gates of opportunities for MSEs. Also, it has ushered in digital documentation, digital identification, and digital verification of MSEs using Aadhar KYC e-process, e-income tax returns and permanent account numbers (PAN), and online data from Ministry of Corporate Affairs to facilitate entire process, totally paperless and on real-time basis. Thus, UNDP strategy of "adopt products and processes" has been effectively used to deal with some of the most daunting regulatory challenges for MSEs to make them inclusive in business in India.

Physical infrastructure

One of the other constraints identified by UNDP for small businesses is inadequate physical infrastructure. This includes lack of road network, undeveloped physical marketplaces, poor communication systems and lack of basic civic necessities like electricity and drinking water. In Indian context, this constraint can be understood in terms of lack of visible physical marketplace for the MSEs where they can display and sell their products and services to consumers. Also, because of limited financial capability, these MSEs are almost unable to advertise their products to attract attention of prospective buyers. They cannot go from office to office to look out for the potential government customers for their products.

GeM adopts UNDP strategy of "adopt products and processes" to tackle some of these constraints of lack of physical infrastructure. GeM is a contactless and virtual marketplace, thus eliminating the need for a physical marketplace for MSEs to sell their products. As entire demand is available and visible on GeM platform, MSEs can do away with the advertising for their products and services for potential government buyers. They need to simply check demand of buyers online and respond to such buyers in their pursuit to do business with government. As this demand is dynamic, MSEs can plan their inventories depending on the volume of orders incoming, rather than maintaining a huge inventory waiting for demand to come in, this saves a lot of hassle and money for them in inventory management in physical space (The True Picture, 2019).

A definite requirement for a system like GeM to be used is a reliable and stable internet connectivity and a certain level of mobile and internet penetration. India, with a 687.6 million internet users in January 2020, and clocking an annual growth of 23% in the number of internet users, has achieved internet penetration level of more than 50%. Also, the mobile penetration level is 80% with a total of 1.06 billion mobile devices in the country in January 2020

(Datareportal, 2020). So, this requirement of GeM is largely met by rapid development in mobile and internet penetration and data access for such MSEs in peri-urban and rural areas too. Further, India has the cheapest call and data cost in the world, and this also has helped mobile and internet penetration to increase rapidly in last few years.

Knowledge and skills

UNDP mentions missing knowledge and skills as a constraint for business from both the point of view of consumers about effective use and benefits of certain products, and producers and suppliers about lack of skills for effective and timely delivery with quality at competitive rates. For the purpose of this paper, I use the UNDP viewpoint for MSEs as producers and small businesses. In Indian context, though other private e-commerce platforms like Amazon, Flipkart and Snapdeal were present in market much before the GeM, participation of MSEs on such platforms as sellers was almost negligible (Centre for Public Impact, 2019). It was the GeM, which proved to be a watershed for such MSEs to participate in e-marketplace.

UNDP strategy of "leverage the strengths of the poor" became a major driver for GeM in India for MSEs. It was because the MSEs with their poor financial capacity could still afford and use cheap mobile and internet connectivity and also, such MSEs could price their products at a much competitive prices due to almost negligible overheads. GeM ensured a paperless, contactless and cashless platform for such MSEs to sell their products and services online.

Similarly, UNDP strategy of "adopt products and processes" was evident on GeM platform which hosts a hands-on training manual in almost all Indian languages to guide first time users of this platform step-by-step to register, identify and verify themselves, offering their products, dynamic and flexible pricing strategies, quoting e-bids, supply support and payment support from the buyers. It was like, anybody, who was an MSE, and who could read and write any Indian language and knew basic mobile operations, could be a part of GeM by this step-by-step online support. Most of such MSEs reinvested their income into upgrading their online infrastructure (Centre for Public Impact, 2019), thus materialising the UNDP strategy of "invest in removing market constraints" for such MSEs to effectively participate in business on GeM leading to their inclusivity in business. Further, Government of India adopted UNDP strategy of "combine resources and capabilities with others" for such MSEs, by providing training for GeM at District Skill Development Centres in all districts, where such MSEs received training on all aspects of GeM and shared their success stories with others. Such trainings are still ongoing and have helped government identify and develop clusters of MSEs collaborating for big orders on GeM as collective suppliers (Centre for Public Impact, 2019).

Access to financial services

UNDP identifies this constraint for small businesses as lack of credit and investment due to lack or poor access of formal banking channels, inability to go for large purchases, ill-equipped to deal with market price shocks, and lack of insurance against sickness, or natural and man-made disasters. In Indian context, these constraints are very much present for the MSEs and more often than not, lead to survival entrepreneurship for such MSEs (Vossenberg, 2016). Lack of exposure to formal credit channels compels these MSEs to seek informal credit at a high rate of interest, squeezing their already meagre operating margins and in long run, driving them out of business due to inability to repay the high cost debt (Governance for Development, 2018).

Unfortunately, access to financial services to MSEs is a major constraint for furthering inclusive business approach, which GeM has not addressed so far. GeM handbook mentions that MSEs need to start on GeM with their seed money and then need to reinvest their meagre incomes into the business to scale up business on GeM gradually and as per their financial capacity (Government of India, 2019). But there is no inbuilt mechanism on GeM platform so far, which links MSEs to formal credit channels in a transparent and easily doable way. Provision of long-term institutional credit to the MSEs, made available online on GeM platform, would go a long way for such MSEs to break even faster and start earning meaningful incomes to come out of the bottom of poverty pyramid (Governance for Development, 2018). One can only hope that to become a truly inclusive e-commerce platform, GeM would sooner than later need to offer such credit linkages for such MSEs to meaningfully achieve inclusivity in business.

Discussion

When we discuss the role of business in development, usually the focus is on big multinational and transnational firms. But most of private sector activity in developing economies is domestic and small, and includes micro, small and medium enterprises (MSMEs). The MSMEs account for about 90% of private sector in most market economies (Sayer, 2006). In Indian context, the MSMEs constitute 95% of total private sector units. There are 1.8 million registered MSMEs in India, and micro and small enterprises (MSEs) constitute 99.7% of these 1.8 million registered units (International Finance Corporation, 2012). Similar percentage of MSEs can be assumed for the estimated 28 million unregistered MSMEs in the country. This shows the importance and significance of MSEs in business in developing countries like India. The core function of a typical market system in a developing economy such as India comprises of exchange of goods and services in an overall regulatory atmosphere. But as is obvious, MSEs by their very nature of being out of formal market system are unable to participate in such system. Here GeM comes in to integrate such MSEs with market system by way of market system development and change. Such government facilitated intervention in market system results in making such markets more inclusive, efficient, sustainable and participative for MSEs, by stimulating growth and expanding access for them within such market systems, leading to improvement in the lives of poor (The Springfield Centre, 2015).

MSEs in India face several constraints to achieve inclusivity in business. Government has employed some of the inclusive business strategies prescribed by UNDP to address some of these concerns, using GeM platform. GeM has been able to positively affect constraints like limited market information, ineffective regulatory environment, inadequate physical infrastructure and missing knowledge and skills for such MSEs by adopting strategies like adapting products and processes, investing in removing market constraints, leveraging the strength of the poor and combine resources and capabilities with others to promote inclusive business for MSEs in India. But, still there are major constraints like restricted access to financial services for these MSEs, which GeM needs to address yet. Similarly, GeM also needs to evolve to engage MSEs in policy dialogue with government as a strategy for inclusivity. Further, some constraints to inclusive business for such MSEs have been better tackled by the GeM using multiple strategies as against some other constraints which have not been tackled that adequately. Based on the analysis so far, I have mapped these strategies and constraints of the GeM on the UNDP strategy-constraint matrix as shown in Figure 5.3 below.

Figure 5.3: Inclusive business strategies employed by GeM to tackle constraints for MSEs

Conclusion

In this paper, I have proposed an alternative approach to inclusive business by focusing on the role of government as an enabler in achieving inclusive business for the MSEs. I have identified various approaches to achieve inclusive business and then justified how the UNDP constraints-strategies matrix framework is the best approach to support my view in this paper and to explain how government has used GeM to positively influence inclusive business in India for MSEs. Then I have discussed the concept and context of inclusive business, government as a development actor, and micro and small enterprises (MSEs) as used in this paper. I have highlighted the case of Government e-Marketplace (GeM) to explain how government has promoted and enabled inclusive business for MSEs in India. I have supported my argument by demonstrating how government, by way of GeM, has employed some of the UNDP strategies to address and tackle some of the market constraints the MSEs face to achieve inclusivity in business. I have mapped such strategies employed by government and the constraints tackled by them on the UNDP market constraints-inclusive business strategies matrix to further my argument. I have also acknowledged the fact that government has been able to remove some of the major constraints to inclusive business for MSEs, as it is yet to address the critical constraint of access to financial services for MSEs. Based on the constraints-strategies mapping and discussion, I sum up by stating that though GeM has been instrumental and has furthered the enabling role of government as a development actor in promoting inclusive business for the MSEs in India, yet, to make it a truly inclusive e-commerce platform, GeM would need to allow for formal credit linkages for MSEs to meaningfully achieve inclusivity in business, and such an opportunity for the MSEs to access long-term and cheap institutional credit would go a long way in augmenting their scale of participation in inclusive business.

VI

MUTUALLY INCLUSIVE ROLE OF GOVERNMENT AND MARKET IN ECONOMIC DEVELOPMENT

Learnings from Green Revolution in India

The issue of market failure versus government failure has been one of the most discussed in development community, with as many critics and advocates of both sides. This issue keeps coming to forefront with every episode of economic slowdown, with government advocates pitching for effective regulatory intervention to tackle such market failures, and market advocates assigning such market failures to unwarranted government intervention in markets. This paper attempts to discuss different dimensions of market failure and government failure and their interactive dynamics. The paper also reviews in brief whether government intervention or actions of market are more likely to derail the economic development and opines that it is the actions of market which are more likely to derail the economic development and government needs to step in to correct this scenario. The paper goes on to suggest that the government failure is the greater risk in developing countries than the market failure, and that well-meaning and well-designed appropriate government intervention is crucial to avoid situation of market failure. To support these viewpoints, I discuss the green revolution in India, as a case study, to explain the interplay of government and market in the process of efficient market functioning and economic development in developing countries. Green revolution is an apt case study in this context, as it depicts how planned government intervention helped in ensuring food security in the country (government success), how market response was less than expected (government non-intervention and market failure) and how the government pitched in to tackle that (government success). The paper concludes by discussing how the mutually exclusive role of government and market in economic development is no more relevant in modern welfare economies and how both actors – government and market, need to join hands and come together in synergy and mutual integration to provide efficient and sustainable delivery output of goods and services. While using the terms 'intervention' and 'action' in this paper, I dwell on the concept proposed by Jamnejad & Wood (2009) that 'intervention' includes 'non-intervention' and 'action' includes 'non-action'.[1] Thus, government intervention includes government non-intervention and market action includes market non-action.

Market failure and government failure: The mechanism

Market failure is the scenario when market fails in efficient distribution and utilisation of the resources leading to deviation from Pareto efficiency (Petru & Alexandru, 2019). In such situation, capacity of market to encourage social action or to rectify inherent dysfunctionalities gets severely limited. Market failure can happen either due to structural distortions of market (affecting the competition adversely) or due to price-mechanism distortions.[2] In the state of Parato optimality, goods and services would be produced till the marginal social benefit equals marginal social cost; but in the event of market failure, the goods with positive externalities are underproduced and those with negative externalities are overproduced (Goodman, 2015). Weisbrod has explained market failure in terms of inherent limitations of market in providing collective goods and services.[3] If such collective goods (and services) are left to market, they would be in perpetual short supply, as consumers would not generate paid demand for such goods (Weisbrod, 1978, p. 66).

Government failure happens when government faces information asymmetry and does not have better information than the market, or when government intervention crowds out or displaces market activity leading to lack of overall improvement (GLA Economics, 2006). Political failure or administrative failure may also result in government failure.[4] Also, though it is widely believed that government intervention would result in more equitable resource distribution, but the fact is that government has poor decision mechanisms available for resource allocation (Cornes & Sandler, 1996, pp. 34–35). The government intervention to correct market failure may not succeed if the intervention is ineffective and detrimental to overall prevailing situation, resulting in government failure (World Bank, 2002).

Government failure – the greater risk in developing countries than market failure

Modern welfare economies need both the market and the government to be functional to achieve economic development. However, for the reasons discussed so far, market failure or government failure may happen, and sometimes even co-exist (Buchanan & Vanberg, 1988). The issue whether market failure or government failure is the greater risk in developing countries needs to be discussed in the context of who, out of market and government, can tackle the failure of itself and also of the other.

The success of market pivots on perfect competition, where the market would self-correct in resource use by way of price information mechanism. But this is too simplified an approach because perfect competition and complete information are, at best, asssumptions rather than reality (Keech, Munger, & Simon, 2012). Therefore, Neoclassical welfare economics justifies government intervention in such markets to achieve a more Pareto optimal resource allocation, suggesting thereby that government can tackle market failure but the market itself cannot tackle its own failure. Shepsle & Weingast have given another dimension to this point. According to them, government intervention in such market failure scenario would be termed as successful only if there is a net improvement in market performance.[5] But it is also true that a market failure scenario may not be able to correct itself without government intervention (Shepsle & Weingast, 1984).

I have discussed in the previous section about the mechanism of government failure. But can market intervention do something to tackle or correct this is a pertinent question. Most of the times, the issues like incomplete information, lobbying, issues of ethics and integrity in the government and public service are created by vested market interests (Plekhanov, 2007). So, it is not practical to expect that the same market interventions, which result in government failure in the first place, can address this failure. This is because vested market interventions are usually a cause of government failure, not its remedy.

Though government failure is not inevitable, yet it could be tackled by better government initiatives in terms of improved responsiveness and efficiency of government. But these initiatives can be taken only by the government itself. Market intervention cannot address government failure by reinventing government initiatives. Whenever government failure happens, the government itself corrects such situation by bringing in policies which improve its credibility and legitimacy (Stiglitz, 2008). Government, which fails to do so, is often replaced by another government only, and not by the market. Thus, market intervention cannot correct government failure, only government intervention can. This goes on to suggest further that government failure is the greater risk in developing countries than market failure.

When market failure happens due to any reasons discussed so far, the private firms go out of business. The same analogy does not and cannot apply to government because the question of government going out of business does not arise (Williams, 2010, p. 213). Government is not subject to the guiding principle of market discipline.[6] This renders the government in dominant position vis-à-vis market in the market failure – government failure matrix, thereby emphasising that government failure is the greater risk than market failure.

The recent collapse of Thomas Cook in the UK is worth mentioning here. This collapse of a private business firm was a typical case of market failure, which left almost 150,000 holidaymakers stranded abroad in various parts of the world. The Civil Aviation Authority (CAA) of the Government of UK launched a massive GBP 520 million Operation Matterhorn[7] to bring back all stranded travellers home within two weeks of the collapse of Thomas Cook, wherein more than 1,000 flights were chartered and operated by the UK government (Makortoff, 2019). This episode shows how government can intervene to tackle any market failure scenario. But the question that should be raised here is: would any private business firm do the same if a government run airline company met with a similar fate? This goes on to support that not only in developing countries, but even in developed countries like the UK, it is the government which comes in to tackle market failure and not vice versa, so government failure would be a real greater risk than the market failure. Though there is always a distinction made between market failure and firms going out of business, yet there is usually an underlying market failure when the firms go out of business.

What is more likely to derail the process of economic development?

For an equitable economic development, it is essential to have a balance between private advantage (and private cost) on one hand and social advantage (and social cost) on the other. As the very nature of market is to maximise private advantage and minimise private cost, more often than not, this leads to disparity between private and social advantage and cost (Coase, 1974, p. 357). In such scenario, action of private sector and market is likely to derail the process of equitable economic development, necessitating the government intervention.[8] Government steps in to overcome this market and private sector induced failure by taxing private goods and incentivising production of collective or public goods (Weisbrod, 1978, p. 66).

In Neoclassical welfare economics, the simple version of market (failure) theory is based on two parts (Keech,

Munger, & Simon, 2012) – one is the assumption that perfect competitive market is the default mechanism for optimal resource allocation; and second is the assertion that market failure consequent to imperfect competition needs government intervention for correction.[9] This theory itself indicates that actions of market (and private sector) are more likely to derail the process of economic development (as perfect competition is a mere thoeretical possibility). Government steps in to correct this market failure and augment economic development by using fiscal and policy tools (Furton & Martin, 2019). In the modern welfare state, the government is expected to play the role of 'night watchman' for the activities which people cannot do by themselves e.g., enforcing contracts (Goodman, 2015). Therefore, when market action leads to market failure and the derailment of economic development process, it is almost natural for the government to step in.

The mechanisms through which the market functions to produce efficient delivery output, are created and provided by the government in almost all cases, mostly in form of policies or regulations (GLA Economics, 2006). In such cases, when market fails to deliver, government has to intervene to halt the derailing of eonomic development process; and to make an improvement in the discriminating market output and outcomes. Further, it is not only the action (failure) of private sector and market which triggers government intervention in the economy, government intervention may even be needed without existence of market failure. In such scenario, appropriate government policy intervention[10] may be needed in order to address discriminating market outcomes (Zerbe & McCurdy, 1999). Appropriate and timely government intervention thus remedies market action and helps prevent market failure, thereby mitigating the derailment of economic development process caused by market and private sector action.

Even in the process of providing for pure private goods, a well functioning market usually faces socio-economic and technological limitations. These limitations can be tackled only by systemic interventions by the government, wherein government needs to provide a direction of change to market and support the process of economic development (Mazzucato, 2013). These systemic interventions of government can transform the system to usher in an enabling environment for ecomonic development process, thereby making it feasible for market to perform (Keller & Block, 2013).

But the rationale for government intervention to prevent market failure may not always work, especially when market does not respond to government intervention in an expected way. Would government intervention lead to improvement in market failure scenario depends upon how the government intervenes in such a scenario. Government may supplement the improvements in market functioning by addressing underlying cause of such market failure leading to derailment of economic development process; or it may try to supplant it by becoming the lead actor in the situation (GLA Economics, 2006). Also, it is important to note that government intervention comes at a cost to the public exchequer. Therefore, there must exist a clearly demonstrable cost – benefit analysis to show that intervention would improve the economic situation and the benefits would exceed the cost (Furton & Martin, 2019). If this is not the case, such intervention is likely to fail leading to government failure. In such situation, though government intervention does not further derail the process of economic development caused by market action, it does not improve the situation either.

Green revolution in India – a case study of government success and market failure

India faced severe shortage of foodgrains in early 1960s due to two successive bad monsoons (1964 and 1965) and resultant widespread crop failure. This shortage became so acute by 1965, that India had to import 10 million tons[11] of wheat from the USA under the PL-480 (Food for Peace) program (CQ Almanac, 1967). To prevent such situation in future, the Government of India launched Intensive Agricultural District Program (IADP) in phases from 1960 to 1968 (Evenson & Mohan, 1974). IADP was rechristened as High Yielding Varieties Program (HYVP) in 1966–67 with the adoption of high yielding varieties of foodgrains. The HYVP coupled with intensive irrigation and intensive fertiliser use was termed as the green revolution in late 1960s and it emerged as the major step in achieving self sufficiency in foodgrains production in India (Swaminathan, 1969). Thus, green revolution program launched by Government of India is a classical example of a scenario when the need of government intervention emerges principally due to the market non-action in case of particular goods (and services) leading to market failure. The green revolution was aimed at tackling two most critical problems of the time – shortage of foodgrains and rural poverty. It is interesting to note how green revolution witnessed various phases – government success in policy intervention to tackle food shortage, government non-intervention to leave poverty reduction to the market and the subsequent market failure to address it, and finally, government success in policy intervention in form of the poverty alleviation programmes. This case study supports the view that in developing countries, government failure is the greater risk than market failure and action (and non-action) of market and private sector is more likely to derail the process of economic development rather than government intervention, which augments and supports the economic development process.

Green revolution and food security – a case for government success

Government action was mandated in the form of policy intervention in agricultural sector in India because private sector and market chose to stay away from agricultural sector, leading to market failure due to non-action of market.[12] Basu (2009) has analysed this scenario in great detail. According to him, the main actors in market, crucial for the success of green revolution, were private investors, who would invest to meet newly created demand of fertilisers, pesticides, irrigation pumps, agricultural implements like tractors and harvestors etc.; and banks, most of whom were in private sector and would meet increasing credit requirement of farmers for adopting green revolution practices. Though, both these actors were reasonably informed and convinced by the government, that green revolution would trigger an intense demand generation of farm and credit imputs, they were still not in a position to make appropriate investment decisions in the agricultural sector. Basu has attributed this non-action to the fact that most of the farmers adopting high yielding varieties were those with land holdings of under two hectares, and their spending capacity to buy inputs and loan repayment capacity was doubtful. This resulted in a situation where private sector and market shied away from agricultural sector leading to market failure (Basu, 2009).[13]

Government intervened in the form of a massive awareness campaign and agricultural extension program to provide information and extension services to farmers right up to village level (Srinivasan, 1979). To tackle the failure of private banks in providing finance to farmers, government intervened by nationalising 14 of India's largest private banks in 1969 and launching the lead bank scheme,[14] resulting in direct government control over these banks (Haque & Verma, 1988). To tackle the problem of providing inputs at reasonable prices, government intervened in the form of substantial subsidies to farmers for purchase of these inputs, but this intervention had a limited success as very few private players actually entered the market to produce such inputs. Government was forced to intervene again by undertaking direct production of these inputs[15] in the state-owned public sector units (Srinivasan, 1979). These timely and appropriate government interventions resulted in increase of area under agriculture by 11% and yield per acre by 61% from 1970–71 to 1996–97 and India became a net foodgrain surplus country in 1998 (Government of India, 1998). Though government intervention is usually linked to failures by market advocates, it needs to be mentioned here that, in the market failure scenario discussed above, green revolution would not be a success in India without government intervention from time to time (Basu, 2009).

Green revolution and poverty alleviation – a case for both government non-intervention and market failure

Reduction of rural poverty was another ambitious objective of green revolution, along with the food security. This objective was based on the the fact that the high yielding varieties had a shorter maturity period, which made it possible for farmers to have multiple crops. It would presumably increase the employment opportunities in the rural areas by providing more labour days to rural poor and farm labourers and would increase wage rate and reduce food price due to increased output, thereby positively affecting their income and directly addressing the rural poverty (Rudra, 1971). Based on this presumption of trickle down, Indian government chose to adopt non-intervention strategy and left the issue of poverty reduction totally to the market. This is a classic case of government non-intervention due to information asymmetry,[16] which Basu has described as 'inaccurate economic prediction of trickle down' by the government (Basu, 2009). But, this expected market induced trickle down did not happen. In fact, number of rural poor (living below poverty line) increased from 31.8% in 1964–65 to 63.1% in 1967–68 (Bardhan, 1970). Rudra has attributed this phenomenon to emergence of large scale mechanisation in rural areas post green revolution, and decline in tenancy cultivation practice, coupled with frequent monsoon failures (Rudra, 1971). This resulted in reduced demand for farm labour and consequently, trickle down did not happen. Thus, government non-intervention was followed by market failure to deliver on poverty reduction front.

Poverty alleviation programs – a case for government success

As I have discussed above, green revolution in India resulted not only in increase of rural povery but also in the income inequalities. In fact, the rural unemploment rose but the farm wages did not rise between 1964–65 and 1967–68 (Bardhan, 1970). It came to be gradually acknowledged by the government by early 1970s, that, poverty reduction cannot be completely left to the private sector and market and a policy intervention was needed. Government chose to actively intervene by launching poverty alleviation programs[17] from 1972 to address the issue of poverty directly. These programs ranged from self-employment generation to wage employment, and were typical of top-down, bureaucracy dependent government intervention. In spite of some shortcomings, these interventions accounted for more than half of the increased incomes of rural poor within a decade of launch (Kochar, 2008). Kochar has reported that the rural poverty levels quickly stabilised in late 1970s and fell from 43.06% in 1977–78 to 37.54% in 1982–83. Thus, green revolution did not reduce poverty endogenously as was presumed initially. Government banked on the idea of trickle down effect and left poverty reduction to the market to tackle, which did not happen. It was government non-intervention to start with, followed by market failure to respond as per the expectations of the government, and ultimately government intervention and success, which resulted in rural poverty reduction in India (Basu, 2009).

Lessons learnt and the way forward

The discussion of green revolution in India above provides some important learning points in the market failure – government failure debate. One, that government intervention does not always fail as is the common belief, and the second, that market does not always succeed as is commonly believed. But, in the modern welfare developing economies, most of the goods and services are neither pure public nor pure private, and such impure goods[18] need both the government and the market for their efficient and sustainable provision (Buchanan, 1966, p. 48). A mixed government and market intervention to adapt to extenalities in such cases is often needed (Mendelsohn, 2003). Therefore, it is not relevant and practical in modern times to argue whether government or market provides better and more efficient goods (and services) (Basu, 2009). In fact, more often than not, the government failure and market failure is intermixed and interlinked (Williams, 2010, p. 213) as was evident during the collapse of Lehman Brothers in the 2007 financial crisis of the USA.[19]

Due to the externalities in the economy, the risk of failure of both government and market is substantial. Given such risk, it is imperative that government intervention be directed to help market perform more equitably and efficiently rather than crowding it out by direct action.[20] Government intervention should be aimed to tackle the cause of any prevailing market failure and not only the menifestations of such market failure, else government intervention to tackle market failure may end up as government failure (GLA Economics, 2006). Government needs to play a role in encouraging appropriate market interventions to avoid market failure scenario by providing incentives so that market is able to adapt to externalities and perform (McCarthy, Canziani, Leary, Dokken, & White, 2001). There is a need to have a judicious mix of the government and the market to have a better output performance rather than pure government or pure market; and the total cost and total risk[21] of providing goods and services by such a hybrid is much less than if such goods and services are provided for by the government or the market alone (Hennart, 1993).

Modern welfare economies have witnessed over the course of 20th century, that there has been a shift from government led – public sector based approach to market led – private sector based approach. Due to this shift, government has transtioned from provider of public services to provider of an enabling atmosphere favourable for market to develop and perform efficiently. This shift in approach is not necessarily a result of government failure, but more so due to changing role of government as facilitator of market (van der Meer & Noordam, 2004). Market failure creates grave impediments in the process of economic growth and government needs to intervene in such scenario by creating a functioning environment to support and promote appropriate market institutions. Thus, it is important to have a mutually inclusive and supportive matrix of government and market institutions for development (Datta-Chaudhuri, 1990).

Conclusion

Economic development process in developing countries is a complex interplay of government intervention (and non-intervention) and market and private sector action (and non-action). In this paper, I give a contextual background of the mechanism of government failure and market failure. Then, I underline that government failure is the greater risk in developing countries because correction and mitigation of government failure is possible by government intervention only. Subsequently, I highlight that actions of private sector and market are more likely to derail the process of economic development and often, government intervention is warranted to put the economy back on track. While discussing the case study on green revolution, I trace how the process of green revolution progressed in India in the 1960s and 1970s with the emergence of government success, market failure and then government success settings in India rural and agricultural sector. I also challenge the two most common beliefs in government vs market debate by emphasising that government intervention does not always fail, and market action does not always succeed. Ultimately, drawing from the lessons from green revolution, I argue that the concept of only government or only market no longer remains relevant in modern welfare developing economies; and both the government and market need to move in a coordinated manner to supplement each other to achieve equitable and efficient economic development and distributional outcomes.

Notes

1. Non-intervention is also an intervention, similarly, not taking any action (non-action) is also an action. These are usually planned strategies in some situations. These strategies are used in areas where the use of force is not possible (Jamnejad and Wood, 2009).

2. Examples of structural market distortions are monopoly, information asymmetry and externalities – both positive and negative. According to Petru & Alexandru (2019), pure monopolistic market situation is exceedingly rare in modern economies and whenever it exists, it is a result of an active government intervention in the form of some regulation. Information asymmetry is the lack of correct and complete information and it affects both the producers and consumers alike.

3. Weisbrod (1978) has defined collective goods (and services) as those which are available to and utilised by all consumers irrespective of the payment for availing these, e.g., a dam. As most of the consumers do not pay for such goods, this would result in low or no production of such collective goods, which otherwise are the real need of the public.

4. Political failure of government happens when vested individual or group interests take precedence over the public interest and public benefit. Administrative failure happens when the public servants face lack of incentive structure or motivation to perform their duties for general public good (GLA Economics, 2006).

5. It is not that government intervention is the panacea for market failure. As the government also faces the limitations of information, government intervention may fail to improve or even deteriorate market failure scenario at times. For a successful intervention, government must have all the relevant information about how market would respond to such intervention, which is seldom the case (GLA Economics, 2006).

6. Government is inherently designed to take collective decisions that affect and apply to everyone, even if these decisions might not be relevant or required by everyone (Williams, 2010, p. 213).

7. The collapse of Thomas Cook was imminent as the UK government had rejected an arrangement to bail out the company from its mounting debts. This itself shows that once the company was about to collapse (market failure), it approached the government for rescue, as happens in many instances of market failure. But in case of government failure, government does not seek any such market bailout initiatives.

8. Coase has explained this using case of British lighthouses (c. 16th century), which were built and operated by the British government as 'public goods' because private sector would not invest in them. The lighthouse was seen as the institutional solution by the government to the problem of market failure (Coase, 1974, pp. 357–376).

9. This assertion is again based on the presumption that the government has well-meaning intention and complete access to full information while taking decisions for Pareto optimal resource allocation.

10. Appropriate government intervention may be in form of taxes, subsidies, incentives or regulations. This intervention is usually a judicious mix of elements like information,

infrastructure, property rights and investment among others (Zerbe & McCurdy, 1999).

11. In 1965, 10 million tonnes of wheat was shipped from the USA in almost 600 shiploads. This amounted to almost one fifth of total wheat production of the USA in 1965, under the Public Law 480 (PL 480) program.

12. As I have already mentioned in my opening remarks of this paper, action includes non-action and intervention includes non-intervention (Jamnejad & Wood, 2009).

13. This market failure was primarily due to incomplete information (Basu, 2009) because investment decisions of private sector are guided by demand perception in future and this information was not available to the private players in 1960s.

14. Lead bank scheme was launched in the same year (1969), wherein each district was assigned a public sector bank as lead district bank, with a priority lending target for agricultural sector, at subsidised lending rate and without the requirement for collaterals. This intervention was made to facilitate easy credit access to the farmers.

15. Government owned public sector units were producing seeds, fertilisers, pesticides and agricultural implements including tractors and harvestors.

16. The assumption was that the growth in farm output would be sufficient for market to take care of output and distribution, requiring no external intervention, meaning, in other words, that market would take care of poverty on its own.

17. Poverty Alleviation Programs (PAPs) is a collective nomenclature for various programs launched from 1972 onwards, such as the Integrated Rural Development Program (IRDP), National Rural Employment Program (NREP), Rural Landless Employment Guarantee Scheme (RLEGS) among others. NREP and RLEGS were merged into Jawahar Rozgar Yojana in 1989.

18. For pure private goods, principles of full excludability (meaning that potential users of such private goods can be excluded form using them by the providers) and full rivalry

(meaning that such private goods can be used only one time by the user on pay basis) apply, but pure public goods are free from both these principles. Examples of pure public goods is biodiversity, of pure private goods is electronic appliances, and of impure goods is the fish in the seas. For more details, refer to Buchanan, 1966, Ch. 4.

19. According to Williams, it was a mix of US government failure to timely intervene and financial market not following the regulations, which caused the collapse of Lehman Brothers in 2007 US financial crisis.

20. Direct government action is likely to fail as government has no price mechanism available for decision making which is available to market. So, government has to rely on cost-benefit analysis mechanism to decide when and how much to intervene.

21. According to Hennart (1993), total cost includes social cost, private cost and coordination cost, the total risk includes the technology risk and diversified risk.

VII

INDIA-IRAN DEVELOPMENT COOPERATION

Opportunities and Challenges of Chabahar Port Project

Nations of the Global South share colonial history and similar development challenges. This connection drives South-South Cooperation amongst them in terms of aid, technology transfer, knowledge and solutions sharing and economic partnerships. There are wide-ranging strategic, economic, diplomatic and political implications of South-South development cooperation not only for donors, but also for the recipients. This paper attempts to present the viewpoint of recipients of development cooperation, in terms of both opportunities and challenges. I discuss these aspects citing the case of Chabahar Port Project in Iran, being developed by India, as per its regional aid policy under South-South Cooperation. To start with, I discuss how India's aid policy is different from traditional aid policy of the North, and even from emerging Southern donors, by being in the ambit of South-South Cooperation driven by its national interests. India has emerged as a major donor in South-South Cooperation. Iran has been an important recipient of India's foreign aid since 1970s. I then briefly cover the motives behind aid program in general and for the Indian aid in Chabahar project in particular, and how these motives create challenges for the recipients of development cooperation. Briefly outlining the Chabahar project, I mention the benefits of this project in terms of opportunities for Iran. I also highlight the challenges this project entails for Iran and how Iran has tried to tackle some of these. I sum up by suggesting that instances of South-South Cooperation bring both opportunities and challenges for the recipients. It becomes imperative for both donor and recipient of development cooperation to find mutual strategic and economic grounds to complete and commission such projects to have a win-win situation.

South-South Cooperation: India as a donor

UNDP visualises South-South Cooperation as a collaboration among countries of Global South as seen in increased South-South trade, FDI, regional integration and technology transfer among other areas (United Nations Development Programme, 2018). India's development cooperation has been labelled as a departure from normative aid framework of Northern donors – OECD (Organisation for Economic Cooperation and Development) and DAC (Development Assistance Committee), because India links it to its strategic economic interests rather than traditional donor principles of democracy, good governance and human rights (Dreher, 2011). India's aid policy is based on the framework of South-South Cooperation reflecting the change in global geographies (Mawdsley, 2010). India's development cooperation is even different from other emerging Southern donors like China and Brazil as it is framed within the South-South Cooperation with historical and nationalist references (Chaturvedi, 2012). India has never treated aid recipient countries in traditional 'donor-recipient' terms (Chanana, 2009), but as 'development partners' (Chaturvedi, 2012).

Whereas traditional foreign aid from North is generally conditional aid, tied to neoliberal preconditions for recipients and targeted to specific social sectors like health and education, Indian development cooperation is extended as untied aid as grants and concessional loans to its aid partners targeted at infrastructure development guided by mutual economic-strategic interests, in recognition of development needs of its aid partners (Mawdsley, 2012). Thus, India's foreign aid policy continues to evolve within South-South Cooperation based on inclusiveness, being demand-driven, mutually gainful, underlined by India's own development experience and contributing to India's rise as soft power (Chaturvedi, Chenoy, Chopra, Joshi, & Lagdhyan, 2014). The Government of India in 2014 rolled out its flagship Neighbourhood Policy, guided by geopolitical and strategic interests, to gain international influence, through targeted partnerships and investments in specific projects in partner countries (Choudhury & Nagda, 2019), to further India's South-South Cooperation. Sometimes, aid principles of India lead to the problems of execution delays because Indian aid program seeks to strengthen institutions of recipient government and technical capacity building, unlike China, which aims for swift project completion without involving recipient agencies or institutions (Srinivasan, 2015).

Chabahar is an apt case of India-Iran development cooperation and represents India's aid principles within the South-South Cooperation, being mutually beneficial for both, with no interference in internal Iranian matters, slated to boost India's position strategically vis-à-vis Pakistan and China, and bringing trade and commerce gains for India (Karthikeya, 2010). The project is funded via the Line of Credit (LOC) and grants component of India's development cooperation program. Though conceived to be mutually gainful, benefits of Chabahar project for Iran outweigh benefits of this project for India (Tanchum, 2014), as I would highlight later. This is in sharp contrast to development cooperation extended by other Southern donors like China, where the aid benefits accrue much more to the donor than the recipient, usually labelled as the exploitative aid policy of such donors to gain from underdevelopment of such recipients (Humphrey & Messner, 2006).

Influence of donor motives on aid recipients – India-Iran development cooperation

Riddell has identified the motives behind why donors give aid. These motives include show of solidarity, historical ties, help in emergencies, help to achieve development goals, providing global public goods, promoting human rights, to further donors' national, political, strategic and commercial interests (Riddell, 2008, p. 92). Though discussed in context of North-South aid, these motives also explain the drivers behind South-South Cooperation. But in reality, the visible narratives of aid usually tend to conceal the real donor motivations behind such programs, these real motives being commercial and geopolitical self-interest, domestic and international interests, national, cultural and racial superiority, and gains in various influence groups like G77 (Mawdsley, 2012, p. 161). In case of Indian development cooperation under South-South Cooperation, solidarity and historical ties were the motives of Indian aid program immediately after its independence (Nigam, 2015). Gradually, these motives have been dominated by India's national, strategic and commercial interests. But, overall, India's development cooperation is rooted in the principles of South-South Cooperation of mutual gain and collective growth opportunities with minimal interference, drawing from India's own development experience (Chaturvedi, 2016).

Indian aid motives behind Chabahar range from historical ties with Iran due to Shia factor,[1] to the regional, strategic and commercial motives. India views Iran as a balancing factor in countering Pakistan and as an access to Afghan markets and beyond, to Central Asia, bypassing Pakistan route for trading (Karthikeya, 2010). India shipped its first wheat shipment to Chabahar in October 2017, signalling the redundancy of Pakistan as an obstacle to India's trade with Afghanistan (Devulapally, 2018). Further, India is projecting Chabahar as a counter to China's Belt and Road Initiative in development of Pakistani port of Gwadar. (Husseinbor, 2016). But, Chabahar project driven by these motives of India has also created unique challenges for Iran. Coupled with Iran's own ambitions of regional domination and balancing Saudi power equation, these challenges have further become complicated for Iran (Basu, 2020).

Chabahar Port is a southern Iranian oceanic seaport located on Gulf of Oman, constituted of two ports – Shahid Kalantari and Shahid Beheshti. Chabahar project holds a central position in India's regional aid strategy under South-South Cooperation (Wolf, 2017). India had agreed in principle to develop and expand Chabahar Port in 2003, but formal agreement for the same was entered into in May 2016 (Tolo News, 2019). India-Iran bilateral relations began in 1950s[2] and progressed to Indian Technical and Economic Cooperation (ITEC) in 1970s (Chaturvedi, 2016). The current Indian Neighbourhood Policy puts Iran as a project specific partner for Chabahar project under "Immediate Neighbourhood" category (Choudhury & Nagda, 2019).

Opportunities of Chabahar Port project development cooperation for Iran

Though driven by India's strategic, geopolitical and commercial interests, Chabahar project is enormously important for Iran too. Chabahar provides a unique opportunity to Iran to achieve regional development and connectivity for relatively underdeveloped Eastern region by development in and around project area, road and rail links from Chabahar to Central Asia and South-East Asia. Iran has built Chabahar-Zahedan highway and is linking Zahedan (capital of Iranian Baluchistan) to Malik (on Afghan border), to connect onwards to Afghan highways. Iran is also constructing Chabahar – Zahedan rail link with Indian aid to connect existing Iranian rail network to Central Asia and Europe (Husseinbor, 2016).

Chabahar holds far-reaching economic opportunities for Iran in terms of trade, investment, business, and revenue. Though India has suspended its oil purchase from Iran,[3] Iran would easily re-enter Indian energy market, when US sanctions are lifted, given India's involvement in Chabahar (Bazoobandi, 2019). Chabahar has attracted substantial international investments from countries, including Commonwealth of Independent States (CIS), Russia, Afghanistan, Pakistan and China worth USD 100 million (PressTV, 2020). This is apart from Indian investment of USD 500 million in developing Chabahar Port and projected investment of USD $20 billion in and around Chabahar (Devulapally, 2018). Chabahar Port would serve as a key revenue source for Iran from tariffs, duties and utility charges levied on port operations, roads, railways and pipelines (Center for Strategic and International Studies, 2018). Chabahar, being out of US sanctions, has emerged as main entry point for trade inflow into Iran, tackling economic downturn during the sanctions to some extent (France24, 2019).

Chabahar is fast emerging as an alternative to Iran's Bandar-e-Abbas Port in Arabian Gulf, which presently handles about 85% of Iranian seaborne trade. A shallow water Port, Bandar-e-Abbas cannot berth standard international 250,000 MT cargo ships. So, incoming Iranian seaborne cargo needs to be offloaded in Dubai, and then re-transported in smaller 100,000 MT ships to Bandar-e-Abbas. This costs Iran millions of dollars and also deepens its dependency on the UAE strategically, as, UAE being a member of the Saudi-led bloc can cripple Iran's seaborne trade anytime under pressure from its allies. Chabahar being oceanic Port, can berth standard international vessels. Therefore, it can wean Iran permanently off the UAE for seaborne trade, tremendously augmenting Iranian clout over Saudi-led bloc (Tanchum, 2014).

Chabahar Port has boosted international stature of Iran vis-à-vis Saudi Arabia in Arabian Gulf and Indian Ocean (Husseinbor, 2016). Iran has started using Chabahar as a major land, air and naval base, stationing its submarine fleet and shipping its arms to Yemenese Houthi rebels from here (Center for Strategic and International Studies, 2018). Iran is leveraging Chabahar to forge stronger naval cooperation with Pakistan, China and Russia, to gain regional naval dominance over Saudi Arabia. Chabahar is a critical link in Iran's ambition to reduce dependency on Suez Canal for cargo transport to Europe. Chabahar lies on the International North South Transport Corridor (INSTC) and South Asia Corridor (SAC), providing major leverage to Iran for regional dominance and a big market for Iranian products (Devulapally, 2018).

In the aftermath of US sanctions, Chabahar has been instrumental for Iran to assert that isolating it diplomatically would not be feasible, given India's involvement[4] in the project (Basu, 2020). This is evident from stand taken[5] by the USA that it did not intend to intervene in legitimate business activities between Iran and India in, around and through Chabahar Port (Bhadrakumar, 2020). This has effectively held good for development activities undertaken in Chabahar region by various other countries including China and CIS, neutralising isolation of Iran in international community to a large extent.

Challenges of Chabahar Port project development cooperation for Iran

As I have discussed before, Chabahar projected is guided by the India-Iran mutual interests and motives. These interests and motives have laid out several challenges for this project for both countries, especially for Iran. India and Iran signed an agreement in May 2016 to develop Shahid Beheshti Port of Chabahar as Phase I, with India provisioning a USD 235 million LOC. But, due to the USA reimposing sanctions on Iran, ongoing works in Chabahar came to a standstill (Roy Chaudhury, 2017). Though Chabahar Port remains out of US sanctions, yet the sanctions have made it risky for companies to invest here. A two-year dispute over whether India would pay duty on equipment imported into Iran further delayed the project (Marlow & Dilawar, 2018). Phase I eventually became operational in December 2017, but release of first tranche of LOC worth USD 150 million was delayed by India, due to alleged violation of LOC terms by Iranian award of few engineering contracts at Chabahar to Chinese firms. This also delayed the taking over by India of Port operations to

December 2018. Phase I has annual cargo capacity of 8.5 MMT (million metric ton), but in 2017, only shipment to reach Chabahar was 15 MT Indian wheat. With a cargo turnover of 2.1 MMT in 2018, most of its capacity and 3-kilometre waterfront remained substantially underutilised (France24, 2019). Business was expected to take off with India taking over operations, but reimposed US sanctions have not allowed that to materialise (Bazoobandi, 2019).

India-Iran bilateral relations are complicated to comprehend (Karthikeya, 2010). India has consistently voted against Iran's nuclear program at the IAEA (International Atomic Energy Agency) yet expanding aid to Iran substantially under its Neighbourhood Policy, guided by national interests, under South-South Cooperation. India, in pursuance of its US foreign policy, has been expanding its ties with Saudi Arabia, but Iran perceives this as siding with Saudi-led bloc and has retaliated by voicing anti-India sentiments on Kashmir issue. Whereas India has always held Iran as its traditional ally due to Shia factor, it has never approved Iranian role in Yemen, Iraq and Syria over the years (Karthikeya, 2010). Iran, on its part, has been toying with Pakistani and Chinese involvement in Chabahar, much to India's disliking, awarding few engineering contracts to Chinese companies, in violation of India's LOC (Marlow & Dilawar, 2018), leading to India holding up project funds. Iran, parallelly, is riding on Chabahar Port to end its international and diplomatic isolation with India's involvement. Thus, Chabahar has become more of a foreign policy tool for India and Iran, than a mere bilateral aid project (Basu, 2020).

As foreign policy strategy, 'Shia' Iran has been traditional ally to 'Sunni' Pakistan, to balance rival 'Sunni' Saudi Arabia, but due to India's involvement in Chabahar project, Iran risks alienating Pakistan. Further, China[6] has been manipulating

Iran to get involved in Chabahar project (Center for Strategic and International Studies, 2018). The consequent stress in India-Iran relations has adversely affected the progress of Chabahar project. US-Iran relations marred by economic sanctions have also impeded the progress of Chabahar project as mentioned previously.

The present moderate Iranian President Rouhani is constantly targeted by his conservative political opponents for issues like economic slowdown and for being soft to India vis-à-vis Pakistan, forcing him to invite Pakistan to participate in Chabahar projects against Indian ambitions (Devulapally, 2018). Another major challenge to Chabahar is the Baluch factor in Iran's internal politics. Chabahar lies in volatile Sistan-Baluchistan province, the stronghold of Baluch nationalists fighting for independence. It has become increasingly difficult for Iranian government to control their insurgency in Chabahar region. Chabahar project has given Baluch insurgents international coverage and attention by repeated attacks on Iranian forces and project workers in Chabahar (Husseinbor, 2016), further hampering the project progress.

Discussion

Development cooperation comes with particular motives of the donors rather than as charity or philanthropy (Riddell, 2008). Indian aid policy centres around declared objective of mutual benefit, with well-conceived motives of commercial and geo-strategic interests for India, but India's development cooperation is much more mutually beneficial than other Southern donors like China (Fuchs & Vadlamannati, 2013). Still, such donor motives give rise to multifarious challenges for the recipients of development cooperation, along with the opportunities. Chabahar project, considered greatly beneficial, has also presented unique challenges for Iran in terms of implementation, which I have highlighted. This project is a typical "aid for trade" project as India aims to develop India-Iran trade, and infrastructure and connectivity required for such trade through this project, inherently reducing the time and costs of trading with Iran (Bhogal, 2016). Chabahar project, at the level of implementation, is substantially different from the usual cases of development assistance under South-South Corporation due to constantly evolving diplomatic-strategic dynamics as we have analysed, both on Iran's domestic and external front, and impacted by India's own commercial and strategic motives behind this project. Chabahar, on one hand, epitomises the high-level traditional alliance between India and Iran to counter the aid and diplomatic hegemony of not only the traditional Northern donors, but also the aggressive Southern donors like China. On the other hand, at project implementation level, these differences from traditional aid characteristics perhaps become more blurred due to ambitious motives of both countries behind Chabahar project. India, as donor of development cooperation, has also faced challenges in this project. Until and unless Chabahar gets fully commissioned, India's strategic, geopolitical and commercial motives behind this project would be at best, partially fulfilled (Marlow & Dilawar, 2018).

Conclusion

Chabahar project has been described as strategic game changer for India and Iran. For India, it is a counter to

China's Belt and Road Initiative (BRI) and involvement in Gwadar Port of Pakistan, both for strategic and trade reasons. For Iran, it is a counter to USA for isolating it internationally, and to Saudi Arabia for arm twisting it in regional powerplay. In this paper, I have given the context of India's development cooperation and how India's foreign aid policy has evolved within South-South Cooperation. I have explained how India's development cooperation differs from the traditional North-South Cooperation and even within South-South Cooperation vis-à-vis other Southern donors like China. Then, I have enumerated the donors' ostensible motives and real motives behind giving aid and how these motives influence the recipients in terms of opportunities and challenges of such development cooperation. I have cited India-Iran bilateral relations and Chabahar Port project as a case of India's development cooperation under South-South Cooperation to support my argument. Then I have underlined the opportunities and challenges this project has brought for Iran as recipient of development cooperation. I sum up by stating that development cooperation under South-South Cooperation not only brings varied opportunities, but also entails serious challenges for the recipients. Both the donors and recipients need to find mutual strategic and economic grounds to gain from such development cooperation mutually.

Notes

1. India, after Iran, is home to second largest Shia muslim population in the world, who have had traditional family and business ties with Iranians. For more information, refer to Karthikeya (2010).

2. Iran sent its expert team to study technical and administrative working of Indian Railways under the Bilateral Program in 1954, followed by Iranian academics coming to India in 1958 for higher studies under the Scholarships Program of India's foreign aid policy. In 1970s, India included Iran as a major partner in its foreign aid program under the ITEC (Indian Technical and Economic Cooperation), to study the feasibility of development of small scale industries in Iran and railways and transit route (road and ports) to Europe (Chaturvedi, 2016).

3. Before the US sanctions made suspend its oil buying from Iran in May 2019, India was the 2nd largest buyer of Iranian oil, buying around 16% of its annual requirement from Iran every year. For more details, refer to Bazoobandi (2019).

4. Iran sees it as quid-pro-quo from India as it had thwarted India's diplomatic isolation in the Muslim world, clamped after Babri Masjid demolition in 1992, when the then Iranian President Rafsanjani visited India in 1995, and this visit practically ended India's diplomatic isolation. Again, in the same year 1995, Iran abstained form voting in the OIC (Organisation of Islamic Conference) led UNHRC resolution against India on Kashmir issue, thwarting the resolution. For more details, see Basu (2020).

5. This statement was issued consequent to the high-level meeting of foreign and defence ministers of the USA and India, in 2+2 format, held in Washington in December 2018.

6. China is the largest foreign investor in Iran, India being the second largest. China is already involved in many infrastructure projects in Iran including the Tehran Metro Rail Project.

VIII

HOW INDIA'S SELF-INTERESTS GUIDE ITS AID POLICY IN FURTHERING SOUTH–SOUTH COOPERATION

India has been involved with foreign aid for a long time, both in the capacity of a recipient as well as a donor. Whereas India has relied on foreign aid since its independence, it also launched its development cooperation program as a donor almost immediately after independence. Its own experience as an aid recipient, coupled with its development experience over the years, has profoundly influenced India's aid policy as a donor towards its development cooperation. India's aid policy has evolved within the framework of South-South Cooperation, based on the idea of solidarity among developing countries of the Global South, sharing common colonial legacy. Since the economic reforms of 1991, Indian aid program has been more and more guided by strategic motives of India's foreign policy. Indian aid has expanded significantly both in geographical coverage and scope. Though this aid program is within the ambit of South-South Cooperation, India's self-interests have been the main drivers of this aid program. Whereas shared colonial, cultural, linguistic and ethnic lineage formed the basis of India's aid policy in the initial years, lately, geo-political and commercial self-interests have become the most important donor motives influencing this aid policy, which is stated to be recipient demand-driven and mutually beneficial.

This chapter presents a descriptive analysis of India's foreign aid policy as a donor in furthering the South-South

Cooperation, based on the guiding factors behind this policy in terms of donor motives of India's self-interests. It argues that though India's aid policy was based on financial-technical assistance and promotion of trade, culture and political cooperation with countries having shared colonial legacy to begin with, it underwent a policy shift in 1990s to become more self-interest based. This chapter explores that although India's aid program has evolved within the overall ambit of South-South Cooperation, being inclusive, unconditional, need-based and mutually gainful, it has been increasing directed by India's commercial, strategic and political self-interests.

The conceptual framework of this chapter is informed by a review of key academic concepts in aid literature and South-South Cooperation including donor motives. After presenting the conceptual setting, I analyse India's aid policy towards its two Southern neighbours – Bhutan in the immediate neighbourhood and Maldives in the extended neighbourhood, to explain how India's self-interests are driving its aid policy towards these two aid recipients. This is illustrated through tracing India's aid canvass for these two countries, their perceived significance for India and motives behind Indian aid for these two. This paper then attempts to explain recipient perception – both popular and political towards Indian aid in both countries. In doing so, it contributes to the extant literature on the South-South Cooperation from India's perspective as a donor and India's donor motives in these two particular cases.

This paper draws from secondary sources to build up and answer the research objective by illustrating that India's aid policy is not ad-hoc but a carefully planned one, evolving over time in tune with the emerging geo-political developments, and guided by India's self-interest motives, which are peculiar to different development assistance partners of India. This study finds that these self-interests range from strategic and geopolitical to commercial, depending upon partner to partner. The study also finds that India as a developing economy and emerging Southern donor, needs to extend foreign aid as a needy donor, to safeguard its self-interests. The study highlights that though Indian aid is mutually gainful, yet the benefits accruing from such aid are skewed in donor's favour. By explaining how these recipients perceive India's aid, both in popular and political ways, this paper contributes to this research gap in the existing literature. This is important because not much attention has been given in the extant literature to how donor motives vary depending on the recipients. Another finding of this paper is that though Indian aid is stated to be untied and unconditional, it is actually limited by the terms and conditions of the aid instruments.

I start by tracing the historical background of India's aid policy and the policy shift in 1990s, and how this policy was extended to immediate neighbourhood and extended neighbourhood. I then set the conceptual framework of the paper by discussion of key concepts including India's aid canvas as a donor. For contextual framework, I choose Bhutan, a land-locked country from India's immediate neighbourhood and Maldives, an archipelago nation, from extended neighbourhood, as these are two countries for which India is the world's largest donor of aid. After explaining the objective and methodology, I mention the limitations of the study. Then I comparatively describe and analyse the India's aid motives for these two countries. I also discuss and analyse the China factor behind India's aid equation with these recipients. This is important because China is aggressively trying to make economic and diplomatic inroads into traditional aid partners of India.

The chapter identifies important policy implications for India's aid program in furthering its own self-interests and goes on to suggest that there is a need to judiciously practice a mix of both hard and soft power in India's aid policy to achieve the desired self-interests of India as a donor. This is because India is still a developing economy and cannot fulfil its donor motives by only leveraging hard economic power with its development partners, like China does. Also, India has been seen in many instances to be involving itself in the internal matters of the recipients and this is proving to be counterproductive in the sense that China is trying to pitch itself as a non-interfering ally at the cost of India. I conclude by recommending the areas of further research in terms of India's development partners in similar geographic settings like Nepal and Sri Lanka as well as in different geographical settings like the African aid partners of India, to understand if India's aid to these partners is also guided by India's self-interests or not. Such further research is also needed to understand the extent to which Indian aid contributes to fulfilment of recipients' self-interests and their development goals.

Historical background of India's foreign aid program

India has been involved with foreign aid for a long time, both as a recipient and donor. India started its aid program as a donor almost immediately after independence. India became a member of the Colombo Plan in 1951, which was initiated as a platform for regional aid and development assistance for South and South-East Asian countries. The Afro-Asian Conference (Bandung Conference) in 1955 initiated Afro-Asian trade, cultural and political cooperation through regional aid on a formal forum. This was labeled as development assistance and thereafter came to be addressed as development cooperation (Dutt, 1980).

Development cooperation as a concept has broader connotation than foreign aid. It not only includes financial assistance, but also capacity building, technical assistance, and promotion of political cooperation, trade and culture within the countries (Chaturvedi, 2012). India launched the Indian Technical & Economic Cooperation (ITEC) program in 1964, to effectively channel its development cooperation under Colombo Plan and Bandung Conference, and expanded it to 50 countries by 1972. Since late 1970s, India's foreign aid program was expanded, both in terms of sectoral coverage and geographical reach (Asmus, Fuchs, & Müller, 2017).

This period of India's foreign aid program had three main features – trilateral cooperation with involvement of non-governmental organisations; focus on supporting less developed immediate neighbours of India; and program-based foreign aid to development partners (Chaturvedi, 2012). Mawdsley has identified the principle motives of India's early development assistance program as energy security (leading to development assistance for hydel projects in partner countries like Bhutan), to push away China (leading to infrastructure development in partner countries like Nepal) and leadership aspirations of the Third World (leading to India's proactive role in the Non-Aligned Movement) (Mawdsley, 2012a, pp. 72–73).

Evolution and policy shift

With the opening of India's economy in 1990s, India's development cooperation underwent a policy shift from

"Third World and anti-West" outlook to a more "self-interested" one (Chaturvedi, 2012). The collapse of the USSR and the end of the Cold War relegated the Non-Aligned Movement into background and made this aid policy shift inevitable. In 2003, the Government of India declared that India would accept only untied aid, reject any future aid by most bilateral donors, and expand grants and project assistance to Highly Indebted Poor Countries (HIPCs) through "India Development Initiative" now on (Government of India, 2003, pp. 22–23). This effectively meant that since 2003, India's bilateral aid relations, as aid recipient, have been limited to the multilateral agencies like G8, European Union (EU), World Bank and the International Monetary Fund (IMF).

India rechristened its development cooperation program under the India Development Initiative (IDI) in the form of "Development Compact", comprising of subsidised credit, concessional loans, Lines of Credit (LOCs), debt relief and technical assistance (Chaturvedi, 2016). As it became essential to have a dedicated execution unit to deliver the Development Compact, Development Partner Administration (DPA) was established by the Government as the nodal and coordinating unit in the Ministry of External Affairs (MEA) in 2012. India's development cooperation, the Development Compact, is now administered by the DPA, with main components as: (1) ITEC program; (2) Lines of Credit (LOCs); (3) trade and investment and (4) grants (Chaturvedi, Chenoy, Chopra, Joshi, & Lagdhyan, 2014). The Development Compact marked the departure of Indian aid program from the OECD-DAC (Organisation for Economic Cooperation and Development – Development Assistance Committee) concept of development assistance by linking trade with concessions and grants, based on mutual gains without conditional ties (Chaturvedi, Chenoy, Chopra, Joshi, & Lagdhyan, 2014).

India has adopted continuously evolving strategic initiatives to conduct its development assistance program in sync with its foreign policy since 2010. Starting with 'Neighbourhood First' policy focusing on immediate periphery, these initiatives include 'Act East' policy emphasising on proactive role in South-East Asia, 'Link West' policy to strengthen ties with Western neighbours and Gulf countries, and 'Indian Ocean Outreach' policy to engage maritime neighbours in security and economic cooperation (MEA, 2016, p. 7). Along with these policy initiatives, India also started placing stronger emphasis on multilateral cooperation based on contribution and sustained participation in international forums like the United Nations (UN), European Union (EU), G20 and BRICS (Brazil, Russia, India, China, South Africa) to collectively tackle global challenges in terms of terrorism, climate change, sustainable development, energy security, food security, cybercrime and space cooperation (MEA, 2018). India is also expanding its development assistance to African countries beyond its traditional relationships within the Commonwealth in an effort to secure access to natural resources as well as serve its broader strategic aims (Ayres, 2017).

Immediate neighbourhood and extended neighbourhood

Since 2000, India has been categorising South Asian region into two categories, based on geographic terms, as a part of its foreign policy – immediate neighbourhood and extended neighbourhood (MEA, 2002). Immediate neighbourhood includes those South Asian nations which share their land borders with India – Pakistan, Nepal, Bhutan and Bangladesh. Extended neighbourhood includes those countries beyond the geographical description of South Asia, which share with India their land and/or maritime borders – China, Myanmar, Indonesia, Thailand, Sri Lanka and Maldives (Kumar, 2016). Further, as a policy revamp in 2004, Indian government broadened the scope of extended neighbourhood and included the Gulf, West Asia, Central Asia, South-East and East Asia, the Asia-Pacific and the Indian Ocean Region (IOR) in this category (Sinha, 2004). Discussing these categories is important to analyse the aid motives of India and whether these motives are the same or different for recipients in different categories, which I would elaborate subsequently.

India witnessed a political change in 2014 general elections. The new government tweaked the flagship Neighbourhood Policy to targeted and specific project-based investments and partnerships in partner countries. The stated objective of this policy was to gain international influence and enhance India's South-South Cooperation (Choudhury & Nagda, 2019), in an open indication of India's self-interest. This Neighbourhood Policy has provided a '360-degree omnidirectional vision' of various military, economic, cultural and ideational opportunities to India in and beyond South Asia, furthering the case of Indian soft power diplomacy by targeted development cooperation program (Scott, 2009). India's foreign aid program is seen as a form of and a tool in developmental diplomacy, designed to encourage growth in fellow developing countries while furthering India's own broader geo-strategic and economic objectives (Amnesty International, 2015). Thus, with this shift, India is projecting itself as a leader of South-South

Cooperation, drawing from its vast leadership experience of Non-Aligned Movement (NAM), and partnering with various multi-lateral development assistance forums like India, Brazil, South Africa (IBSA) and Afghanistan Donors Group among others (Agrawal, 2007).

Global South and South-South Cooperation

The concept of Global South, as differentiated from the Global North, emerged in the post-Cold War era. Separation between Global South and Global North is not geographical, as many parts of the world included in Global South are situated above the equator. The term Global South has been employed to refer to those areas of the world which historically faced racism and colonialism by the developed powers of the North. In post-colonial times, the term Global South has emerged as a political movement against colonial hegemony of the Global North. Thus, the concept of Global South is relational to the hegemonic Global North. But the Global South is not a homogenous spatial concept. It includes varied and multiple political, cultural and economic areas, with wide ranging inequalities, income disparities and political structures, and these factors give rise to power imbalances in the Global South (Murrey, 2019, pp. 64–66).

The idea of South-South Cooperation emerged as a political movement in the Global South in order to break free from economic domination of Global North and asymmetrical power equations arising from the traditional Northern aid. This idea gained momentum post-World War II with the Bandung Conference (1955) and New International Economic Order of 1960s and 1970s, and culminated with the evolution of BRICS (Brazil, Russia,

India, China and South Africa) and IBSA (India, Brazil, South Africa) blocs. Thus, South-South Cooperation which started as a political decolonisation process, has expanded to solidarity in economic and cultural spheres (Ndlovu-Gatsheni & Tafira, 2019, p. 127). The UNDP visualises the South-South Cooperation as a collaboration of countries in the Global South in political, social, economic, cultural, environmental and technical domains. This has been evident in South-South trade, FDI, regional integration, technology transfer and sharing of solutions among other exchanges (United Nations Development Programme, 2018). The South-South Cooperation got a tremendous boost in 2008, when the Overseas Development Assistance to developing countries substantially declined due to global economic crisis. This gap was partially filled by the middle-income countries of the Global South, who emerged as the Southern aid providers (from being Northern aid recipients), for the low-income countries (Aneja, 2019, p. 145).

How South-South Cooperation is different from the traditional Northern aid

There are major differences between the aid policies under the South-South Cooperation and the so called traditional Northern aid of Development Assistance Committee (DAC) of the Organisation for Economic Co-operation and Development (OECD). These differences arise due to peculiarities associated with the Southern donors. The Southern Donors have large populations and economies, but their economic development level is less than the DAC donors, leading to influence on their aid motives. South-South Cooperation is rooted in the philosophy of non-interference in the domestic affairs of aid recipients. It is not aligned and bound by the aid principles and regulations prescribed by the DAC (2005 Paris Declaration on Aid Effectiveness), but instead guided by the freedom to push donors' own national interests through aid activities, usually commercial motives. Further, South-South Cooperation follows dual objective of mutual benefit and lack of policy conditionalities, rather than the DAC objectives of poverty reduction and conditional aid (Asmus, Fuchs, & Müller, 2017). South-South Cooperation is based on "developing country identity", development experience in similar context and treating the aid recipients as partners in cooperation with mutual benefits, as against the typical DAC donor-recipient relationship (Mawdsley, 2012b). Most of the aid under South-South Cooperation is focussed on sustainable individual projects in partner countries as against the DAC focus on long-term debt model (Mwase & Yang, 2012). Aid partnership under South-South Cooperation is aligned with Bandung principles, without any pressure or interference in internal affairs of recipients, and totally premised on the recipients' requirements of aid projects, based on demand-driven approach (Nigam, 2015).

Motives of donors behind giving aid

Whether it is North-South aid or South-South aid, the principles of aid have been traditionally decided by the donors' motivations to provide such aid. On the donor motivation spectrum, these principles can be arranged between two extremes – self-serving "mercantile" motive on one end and morality-humanity motive on the other (Gulrajani & Calleja, 2019). According to Riddell, such donor motives range from historical ties, show of solidarity, help in achieving development goals, helping in emergencies, promoting human rights, providing global public goods and national, political, strategic and commercial interests (Riddell, 2008, p. 92). Though Riddell's work has been on traditional Northern aid, these motives apply to the South-South Cooperation too. The aid may look like philanthropy or charity on the outside, but the visible narratives of aid usually conceal the actual motives of donors behind extending such aid, and can range from domestic and international self-interests, geopolitical and commercial self-interests, cultural and racial superiority, to the implied gains in influence groups and international hierarchy like in the Group of 77 (G77) (Mawdsley, 2012a, p. 161). Thus, as far as the motives of geopolitical and commercial interests are concerned, the aid allocation by traditional Northern donors and emerging Southern donors appears to be guided by similar principles (Dreher, Fuchs, & Nunnenkamp, 2013).

India's development assistance and South-South Cooperation

I have traced the historical background of India's foreign aid program above. Though India has been the largest recipient of foreign aid, receiving in excess of USD 4.5 trillion between 1960 and 2015 (OECD, 2017), yet India initiated its outward foreign aid program almost immediately after independence, guided by the then foreign policy initiatives. Initially shaped by shared colonial history and show of solidarity with its aid partners, India's foreign aid policy has evolved within the ambits of South-South Cooperation, based on six pillars which give it a unique concept. These are: (1) sustainable and inclusive; (2) drawing from its own development experience over the years; (3) need-based; (4) unconditional; (5) mutually gainful; and (6) to support India's rise as soft power (Chaturvedi, Chenoy, Chopra,

Joshi, & Lagdhyan, 2014). India's aid policy is based on the framework of the South-South Cooperation reflecting the change in global geographies (Mawdsley, 2010). With the change in political regime in 2014 in India, the flagship "Neighbourhood Policy" was launched to gain international influence, through targeted partnerships and investments in specific projects in partner countries, to further India's South-South Cooperation, gradually reducing the ITEC component of the IDI since last half decade (Choudhury & Nagda, 2019). India's development cooperation has been focussed on two geographical regions – South Asia and Africa, within the horizontal South-South Cooperation framework (Asmus, Fuchs, & Müller, 2017).

India as a needy donor

With the economic reforms of 1991, India embarked on a trajectory of rapid economic growth to become one of the fastest growing economies of the world (Basu, 2008). India's nominal GDP at current prices in 2019 has been estimated at around USD 3 trillion, making it the 5th largest economy in the world (IMF World Economic Outlook, 2019). Despite this economic progress, India continues to be concerned by problems of chronic poverty, malnourished children, poor human development indices and regional underdevelopment (Banerjee, 2010). On one hand, India received more than USD 4.5 trillion in foreign aid between 1960 and 2015 (OECD, 2017) becoming the largest recipient of foreign aid in the world, and on the other, has been emerging as an important donor and actor in South-South Cooperation. India has become a net foreign aid donor since 2016, which means that foreign aid from India has exceeded foreign aid to India. In 2015–16, India gave USD 1.1 billion in foreign aid and received USD 300 million as foreign aid (MEA, 2018). This phenomenon of India being a donor in spite of still being a developing country is puzzling, but can be explained by analysing the motives driving India's development cooperation program, assigning the status of a "needy" donor to India (Fuchs & Vadlamannati, 2013). Equally interesting is the fact that, in 2010, twenty-three development partner countries of India had more per capita income than India in terms of GDP per capita and purchasing power parity with year 2007 as base year (Dreher, Fuchs, & Nunnenkamp, 2013).

India's "need" to make development cooperation available to its development partners is driven by commercial and political self-interests; this is reflected often in the voting arrangement in UN proceedings (Abraham & Samuel, 2016). India's foreign aid program seeks to fulfil certain needs and is seen as a foreign policy tool to achieve these. There are instances to support this need fulfilment strategy through aid; for example, Zambia, an African development partner of India, supported India during the nuclear tests of 1998 and officially recognised Jammu and Kashmir as part of India in 2003 (Lafargue, 2006). India needs to look for new overseas markets for its ever-increasing trade and commerce, and this need is also taken care of to a large extent as the development partners provide access to their markets and natural resources to India as a quid pro quo (Kragelund, 2008). Dutt (1980) has identified five need elements, which India seeks to fulfil through its foreign aid program. These include need to improve bilateral relations and mutually gain from them, need to improve India's international stature and image to gain in international affairs, need to gain influence over the aid recipient countries, need to maintain stability in recipient countries to gain from the Indian investment there and the need to incentivise recipient's policy by providing need-based aid. These elements also explain the reason for India's development cooperation to take into account the partner countries' concerns too so as to gain their support for the aid program and the needs this aid seeks to fulfil (Dutt, 1980). For India, the needy donor, the self-interest is much more important driver and motive behind giving aid, than in case of the rich Northern donors (Fuchs & Vadlamannati, 2013).

India's national interests and aid motives

As I have mentioned before, solidarity and historical ties from colonisation era were the motives of India's foreign aid policy under the South-South Cooperation since its independence (Nigam, 2015). India's aid program was decentralised and fragmented to begin with, and got consolidated with the launch of ITEC in 1964. Coupled with the Special Commonwealth African Assistance Program (SCAAP) of the 1970s, it touched 161 countries globally by the end of 2010; its main components being, consultancy, training, experts and students exchange and study program, technology and equipment, and humanitarian aid (Mawdsley, 2010). The size of this program reached USD 1.3 billion in 2016–17, adding up to 54% of 2016–17 annual budget of the Ministry of External Affairs (MEA). Apart from this aid, LOCs worth USD 16.9 billion were allocated to the development partners (MEA, 2018). This growth has been in tandem with the growing economy and international presence of India since last three decades, expanding both in geographical reach and sectoral coverage (Chaturvedi, 2012). This also had an effect on the aid motives for India which gradually expanded to cater to self-interests, guided by trade, security and leadership aspirations at global level, and not just limited to the Global South (Mawdsley, 2012a, pp. 72–73). Coupled with the emergence of India as a net donor of foreign aid since 2003, this led to the "reinvigoration of the SSC in a new form" (Chaturvedi, 2012b).

India's development cooperation has been termed as a deviation from the traditional Northern normative aid framework. Whereas aid from Northern donors – OECD (Organisation for Economic Cooperation and Development) and DAC (Development Assistance Committee), is led by normative principles of human rights, good governance and democracy, India has been following its strategic and economic interests in its aid program (Dreher, 2011). Traditional Northern aid is generally bundled with "neoliberal preconditions" for recipient countries, targeting specific social sectors such as health and education. India's development cooperation, on the other hand, is offered untied in the form of grants and soft loans for aid partners targeting specific infrastructural development projects, in tune with the partners' demands and mutual economic-strategic gains (Mawdsley, 2012b). Framed within the South-South Cooperation with historic and nationalistic background, India's foreign aid policy is also a departure from the other Southern Donors like China and Brazil. Rather than engaging with aid recipient nations only on traditional donor-recipient equation, India has always held and treated them as development partners (Chanana, 2009). India's foreign aid program seeks institutional strengthening and capacity building for its development partners, this is unlike China, which practically leaves recipient institutions out of project implementation and executes the aid projects by its own machinery (Srinivasan, 2015).

As an official policy, India's development cooperation is demand-driven, unconditional and untied, guided by mutual gain and within the horizontal South-South Cooperation framework, but has been exceedingly driven by the commercial, strategic and political self interest. This has been evident by the fact that those development partner countries, who have strong commercial and trade relations with India and align with India in the United Nations General Assembly receive significantly more aid (Abraham & Samuel, 2016). This is in line with India's long standing strategic ambition to gain a permanent seat in the United Nations Security Council (UNSC) and increased representation and quota in the IMF to gain more say in economic scenario at international level. India increasingly visualises itself as the link between the Global North and Global South in bodies like G20 (Chaturvedi, Chenoy, Chopra, Joshi, & Lagdhyan, 2014).

India's foreign aid canvass

South Asia and Africa are the two geographic regions which are prioritised by India for development cooperation. The major development partners in South Asia being Bhutan, Sri Lanka, Afghanistan, Nepal and Bangladesh and in Africa being Nigeria, Ethiopia, Ivory Coast, Mozambique, Sudan and Syria (OECD, 2017). Majority of this aid is allocated to energy generation and supply, storage and transport sector, industry, water supply and sanitation (Tierney, 2014). The MEA prepares an Outcome Budget every year which makes a mention of the quantum of India's development cooperation allocation to the development partners, inclusive of all components of the aid, collectively labeled as the Technical and Economic Cooperation (TEC) outlay. The TEC outlay in the latest Outcome Budget Document of the MEA (which is available for year 2016–17) is shown below in Table 8.1.

Table 8.1: Principal beneficiaries of India's development cooperation

TEC Outlay	RE* 2015–16	BE# -2016–17 (*Proposed*)
Bhutan	5612.69	5490.00
Afghanistan	682.94	520.00
Nepal	300.00	300.00
African countries	200.00	290.00
Mongolia	7.50	5.00
Sri Lanka	500.00	230.00
Myanmar	154.00	400.00
Eurasian countries	20.00	20.00
Bangladesh	213.79	150.00
Maldives	213.00	40.00
Latin American countries	15.00	15.00
Others	524.57	447.82
TOTAL	8443.49	7907.82

Source: MEA Outcome Budget 2016–17 (MEA, 2016, p. 11)
* RE – Revised Estimates; # BE – Budgetary Estimates

As is evident from the above Table, almost 90% of India's aid goes to its South Asian development partners and Bhutan has been India's biggest development partner in terms of aid allocation. Bhutan shares its borders with India and India categorises Bhutan in "immediate neighbourhood" category of its foreign policy. (MEA, 2018). Maldives is another South Asian development partner of India but it is geographically distant from India and is categorised in the "near abroad" category (Chanana, 2009). India is the world's largest aid provider to both Bhutan and Maldives, in real terms (Amnesty International, 2015).

Understanding India's aid program

In its foreign policy and development assistance program, India has always remained a fierce advocate of its policy independence; in so much so that it has generally taken a cautious approach to formal alliances and global consensus (Ayres, 2017). This has enabled India to pursue its development assistance program, as a donor, without any external influence on such assistance program. This has been evident during trade negotiations, where India has bargained hard for improved trade and economic alliances, but trodden carefully on the issue of providing Indian market access to the trade partners. In most of the cases, such trade and market access agreements have been entered into with India's development partners. Thus, India's self-interests have always remained at forefront in its foreign policy and development assistance program. Ayres (2017) refers this stance as a shift from 'reflexive non-alignment' to 'strategic autonomy', with policy independence as the underlying principle of its aid motives. Due to this, India has been able to forge aid relations independent of any block or group of aid providers. India's development assistance is clearly a sub-set of a larger set of foreign-policy goals, ensuring energy security and new markets for an expanding economy and bolstering geo-strategic ties with key development partners.

For India, the needy donor, self-interest is an important motive and driver behind its aid policy (Fuchs & Vadlamannati, 2013). But, are these motives different for different development partners or are similar; does self-interest manifests in different forms for different partners? Next question which arises here is what exactly are these interests which India seeks to fulfil by providing aid? These interests could range from strategic, geopolitical, commercial, trade and investment to natural resources. But are these interests carefully planned or just ad hoc? Are these static or evolving with time? And are they general or differ from partner to partner? Are these interests truly mutually beneficial and gainful or skewed towards India's gain over the recipients? And importantly, how do the partners perceive these interests of the donor India? There is not enough evidence available in the existing literature to answer these questions, as the aid literature is replete with general aid motives and aid principles of the donors.

India is the world's largest aid provider to both Bhutan and Maldives, in real terms (Amnesty International, 2015). As is seen from Table 8.1, Bhutan is the biggest development partner of India in terms of its aid allocation. Outside the immediate neighbourhood, Maldives receives the biggest chunk of foreign aid, more than all the African development partners of India combined. Bhutan is land-locked and Maldives is surrounded by Indian ocean. This would give a perspective of India's aid to both these countries, one in the immediate neighbourhood and another near-abroad. Also, these two cases provide an interesting insight into India's aid interests in geographical terms. This becomes relevant here, as not much attention has been given to whether and how donor-specific motives vary depending on the recipients.

India-Bhutan development cooperation

Though Bhutan was a protectorate of British India since 1910, yet development assistance to Bhutan from India started from 1949, when the basic framework of Indo-Bhutan development cooperation was laid down by the 1949 Treaty of Friendship and Cooperation between the two neighbours. I have given a glimpse of India's aid quantum to Bhutan earlier. Now, I will discuss the major areas of this cooperation.

India has extended financial assistance to Bhutan's Five Year Plans since their inception in 1961. For the 11th Plan period (2013–18), this outlay of Indian aid has been INR 5,000 crore, of which INR 3,650 crore is in the form of project assistance in health, education, industry, urban development, roads and energy sectors; and INR 850 crore is in the form of grant (MEA, 2016). Bilateral trade is another important sector of mutual cooperation. India is Bhutan's largest trading partner. In 2018, 82% of Bhutan's imports were from India and 90% of Bhutan's exports were to India, a major chunk of this being hydropower. These figures are shown in Table 8.2 below.

Table 8.2: India-Bhutan bilateral trade

Year	Indian exports to Bhutan* (Bhutanese imports from India)	Indian imports from Bhutan* (Bhutanese exports to India)
2013–14	4,389	2,898
2014–15	4,785	3,180
2015–16	5,374	3,180
2016–17	5,528.5	3,205
2017–18	5398	3162
2018–19#	2978.5	1340

Source: MEA, 2019 (* All figures in INR crore, # 6-months from January 2018–June 2018)

To boost bilateral trade, both countries have established a free-trade regime since July 2017, allowing for trade in local currency and duty-free Indian transit for Bhutanese exports to other countries (MEA, 2017).

In the specific project based development assistance category, hydropower is central to Indo-Bhutan economic cooperation. India has initiated to develop 10,000 MW of hydropower in Bhutan and import the surplus electricity. Three hydropower projects at Tala, Kurichhu and Chukha have been completed with a commissioned total capacity of 1416 MW. Four other projects are in progress for commissioning by 2021–22. Hydropower projects in Bhutan are cited as an example of mutually beneficially win-win cooperation for both countries (MEA, 2017). On one hand, these provide the aid donor India with a reliable source of inexpensive and clean electricity, on the other, generate significant export revenues for the recipient Bhutan, cementing mutual economic integration.

Education and training is another important sector for Indo-Bhutan cooperation. Approximately 4,000 Bhutanese students every year come to India at various levels of studies on scholarships such as the Government of India Undergraduate Scholarship, Nehru-Wangchuk Scholarship, Ambassador's Scholarship, Indian Council for Cultural Relations Aid-to-Bhutan Scholarship. Under ITEC Training Program Scheme, Government of India provides training to Bhutanese nationals for upgrading their technical, business and administrative skills. Under the Military Cooperation Program, a 2,000 strong Indian Military Training Team (IMTRAT) is permanently based in Western Bhutan to train the ranks of the Royal Bhutan Army (MEA, 2017).

Significance of Bhutan for India – India's donor motives for Bhutan

Bhutan's importance for India arises due to its geographical setting. A Himalayan Kingdom, it acts as a buffer between India and China. It is geo-strategically vital for India to secure Bhutan's Western border from any Chinese attempt to alter or realign it, because after the annexation of Tibet by China, Western Bhutanese territories have been directly exposed to Chinese borders. Though India's aid relations with Bhutan were conceived on mutual friendship basis, backed by the Friendship Treaty of 1949, these relations have been increasingly shaped by regional security dynamics since the Sino – Indian war of 1961 (Ramachandran, Hariharan, & Mehta, 2018). In the last six decades, the China factor has become the underpinning factor in these relations. China has been trying to gain formal inroads into the economic-diplomatic sphere with Bhutan. India perceives these efforts to have grave implications for its national security. By strengthening its bilateral relations with Bhutan in terms of development cooperation, India has tried to thwart such Chinese attempts (Stratfor, 2018).

Bhutan also holds immense economic significance for India. It is a ready market for Indian commodities and an attractive venue for Indian investment in various projects. Further, India has identified the Bhutanese potential as a source of hydropower and thus looks up to Bhutan for its energy security in terms of cheap hydropower developed with India's assistance (Stratfor, 2018). Also, a stable and peaceful Bhutan has an important role to play in India's internal security, so that not only the Indian investments there remain safe, but also, there is no possibility of Bhutanese soil being used as a safe heaven for anti-India activities and anti-India groups like the United Liberation Front of Assam (ULFA), National Democratic Front of Bodoland (NDFB), Bodo Liberation Tigers Force (BLTF) and Kamtapur Liberation Organisation (KLO) among others. After the Operation All Clear of 2003 by the Royal Bhutanese Army to wipe out the training camps of these groups from Bhutanese soil, India has keenly made sure that these groups are not allowed by Bhutan to reset their camps there (Stratfor, 2018).

Mutually beneficial development cooperation

I have discussed earlier how India's development cooperation under the overall ambit of South-South Cooperation is based on the principle of mutual gain. Indo-Bhutan development cooperation is described in the Indo-Bhutan Friendship Treaty as 'special', 'exemplary' and 'mindful of each-other's concerns'. These concerns have been described as Bhutan's sovereignty and India's security (MEA, 2007). In fact, the Friendship Treaty of 2007 has brought more equality in these relations, based on 'mutual development needs', as Bhutan no longer requires to be guided by India in its foreign affairs or seek its approval on arms purchases from third parties. In return, Bhutan has not yet accepted the Sino border deal of 1996, which envisages exchange of Jakurlung and Pasamlung Valleys (Chinese territory) with the Doklam plateau (Bhutanese territory), thus safeguarding India's interests on the Western Bhutanese border (Ramachandran, Hariharan, & Mehta, 2018).

The recipient's perception: How Bhutan perceives Indian aid

Since 2010, the trust element in Indo-Bhutan relations has been dwindling. There have been instances when Bhutan has been categorical in its stance against perceived Indian interference (Ramachandran, Hariharan, & Mehta, 2018). A glaring example of this was in 2012–13, when despite

Indian resistance, the Bhutanese Prime Minister met his Chinese counterpart on the sidelines of the Rio Summit in 2012. Just before the Bhutanese general election of 2013, India suspended its fuel subsidy to Bhutan. The ruling party lost the elections, apparently over the issue of public outcry against the steep hike in fuel prices (Bhutan News Network, 2015). This generated negative perception about India's intentions among the Bhutanese people (Dikshit, 2016).

Lately, the Bhutanese media have started mentioning Indian aid as generating 'jobless growth' and 'economic bubble', which may burst anytime. The general sentiment is that Indian aid ultimately flows back to India and has no spiral effect in Bhutan (Stobdan, 2017). Stobdan (2017) has also noted that, there is an evolving sentiment that Indian aid led hydropower projects are being driven by India'a energy needs, as the grant component for these projects has been shrinking and Lines of Credit (LOCs) component is gradually increasing, which entails an interest component as against pure grant, which comes without any interest or repayment liability.

To sum up, India-Bhutan development cooperation, initially based on shared colonial history and solidarity based on cultural and historical ties, has developed within the pillars of South-South Cooperation; being inclusive, based on India's own development experience, need-based, mutually gainful and furthering India's soft power (Chaturvedi, Chenoy, Chopra, Joshi, & Lagdhyan, 2014). Lately, the motives behind such aid, identified by Mawdsley as true donor motives of domestic and international self-interests as well as the geopolitical and commercial self-interests (Mawdsley, 2012a, p. 161) have been driving this development cooperation policy of India towards Bhutan, leading to the recipient perception issues as discussed above.

Indo-Maldives development cooperation

Maldives and India share religious, linguistic, ethnic and cultural links since the days of British colonisation. When Maldives became independent from British rule in 1965, India was among the first few countries to recognise Maldives as a sovereign independent nation (MEA, 2014). I have given a glimpse of India's aid quantum to Maldives earlier. Now, I will discuss the major areas of this cooperation.

India's development cooperation to Maldives is centred around specific project-based aid. India has established some of the leading institutions of Maldives under the projects category, including the Indira Gandhi Memorial Hospital (IGMH), Faculty of Engineering Technology (FET), Faculty of Hospitality & Tourism Studies (FHTS) and Maldives National Police Academy (MEA, 2014). India has also extended aid for relief projects to Maldives many times, notably in 2005, when an aid of INR 10 crore was provided as relief post-2004 tsunami, followed by USD 100 million assistance as relief towards tidal surges of 2007. India has undertaken to construct 485 housing units in Maldivian capital Male via the LAC route worth USD 40 million. India has also financed a USD 5.30 million project for Technology Adoption Program in Education Sector in Maldives on grant-in-aid basis (MEA, 2014).

India is Maldives' 4th biggest trade partner, after UAE, China and Singapore. India and Maldives entered into a Preferential Trade Agreement (PTA) in 1981 to increase the bilateral trade in essential commodities. To further boost the exports, India in 2011 released 3-year quota for export of essential commodities to Maldives, removing the restrictions for export of such items. India-Maldives trade now stands at USD 289 million in 2018–19 (MEA, 2019).

Wheras the Indian exports to Maldives have increased by almost 170% in the last five years, the corresponding figure for Maldives is stagnant during this period. The bilateral trade between the two countries is heavily skewed in India's favour at present (MEA, 2019). The figures have been shown in Table 8.3 below.

Table 8.3: India-Maldives bilateral trade

Year	Indian exports to Maldives* (Maldivian exports to India)	Indian imports from Maldives* (Maldivian imports from India)
2013–14	154	12.3
2014–15	170.6	2.9
2015–16	225.82	3
2016–17	275.5	1.6
2017–18	286.94	2.86
2018–19	286.18	2.81

Source: MEA, 2019 (*All figures in USD million)

Capacity building and skill development is another area of India-Maldives development cooperation. India has been offering scholarships to almost 100 Maldivian students each year at various levels of education in India like Indian Council for Cultural Relations Scholarship, SAARC (South Asian Association for Regional Cooperation) Chair Fellowship, ITEC Scholarship, Medical Scholarship and Technical Cooperation Scheme of Colombo Plan Scholarship. Also, India has been training Maldivian bureaucrats and diplomats (MEA, 2014). India also commissioned the India Culture Centre in Male in 2011, to conduct training courses in yoga, dance and classical music, in an effort to strengthen the cultural roots of India-Maldives relations.

Significance of Maldives for India – India's donor motives for Maldives

Maldives significance for India arises due to its geo-strategic location in the middle of the Indian Ocean. Maldives is an archipelago only 300 miles from the southern Indian coast. Due to its strategic location, Maldives straddles major Sea Lines of Communications (SLOCs) of the Indian Ocean. Also, it is close to Deigo Garcia – the US Central Command Base. Maldives being a Sunni country, maintains close relations with the UAE and other Islamic gulf nations (MEA, 2019). These factors give rise to peculiar Indian motives for development cooperation for Maldives. One of India's primary motives for this aid is the domination of the Indian Ocean Region (IOR), and this is not possible without active Maldivian support. Also, it is in India's interest to maintain political stability and keep fundamental religious forces at bay in Maldives to safeguard its 25,000 strong diaspora and high value Indian investments (Kumar, 2016). Due to ever expanding Chinese influence in India Ocean Region because of the Belt and Road Initiative (BRI), Maldives has become all the more significant for India. India also views Maldives as economically significant due to Indian exports potential to Maldives. Political stability in Maldives is highly important for Indian internal security so as to prevent the use of Maldivian soil for any possible sea-based attack attempts on India.

Mutually beneficial development cooperation

I have discussed how India's development cooperation under the overall ambit of South-South Cooperation is based on the principle of mutual gain. India-Maldives development cooperation is not an exception to this. It is in India's interest to have deep comprehensive engagement with Maldives so that it remains politically, economically and strategically stable and bolsters India's standing in the Indian Ocean Region (IOR). Maldives gains by this cooperation because it sees in India a strategic partner capable of guaranteeing its internal stability and security. This has been evident in 1988 Maldivian coup against the then Maldivian President Gayoom, when India launched Operation Cactus to save the Gayoom government (Kumar, 2016). During the visit of the Maldivian External Affairs Minister, Abdulla Shahid, to New Delhi in 2019, both the sides reiterated that India's 'Neighbourhood First' policy and Maldives' 'India First' policy, based on friendship and trust, strengthen a mutually beneficial partnership which is dynamic and multidimensional (The New Indian Express, 2019).

The recipient's perception: How Maldives perceives Indian aid

Since the regime of President Gayoom, Maldives claims to follow "India First" foreign policy, and his predecessor – President Nasheed continued it. But this approach underwent a sea change during the regime of President Waheed, who raised an issue about India interfering in Maldivian internal affairs on the pretext of preserving democracy (Pattanaik, 2019). This was evident when the Waheed Government terminated the Indian infrastructure major GMR Group contract to develop the Male airport unilaterally. This trend has continued even in the regime of President Yameen, who has openly supported Sino-Maldives relations at the cost of Indo-Maldives cooperation. In fact, as the experience of the last decade shows, rather than the ruling dispensation, it is the opposition in the Maldives, which has always looked up to India for political settlement with ruling party and protecting democracy in Maldives. Though India's aid remains important for Maldives, the Chinese aid quantum is too much to ignore. The present Solih regime has already started talking about refashioning and rebalancing Maldivian foreign policy, to accommodate both China and India, to the best interest of Maldives (Bhatia, 2018). On one hand, India is trying to protect the opposition in Maldivian political space, and on the other, it is trying to boost its fledgling association with the Maldivian ruling dispensation to ensure political stability in the archipelago nation. These two objectives of India's development cooperation with Maldives seem to be at cross-purposes with each other (Pattanaik, 2019). The same opposition, which has sought India's support repeatedly in the past, has been cosying up to China when in power, and this has been evident many times in the past (Bhatia, 2018).

To sum up, India-Maldives development cooperation has its roots in the shared colonial, cultural, linguistic and ethnic history, and has taken shape within the ambit of South-South Cooperation being need-based, mutually gainful and furthering India's presence in Indian Ocean Region. Underlying these principles are India's self-interests, such as geo-strategic and commercial, which have led to this evolving development cooperation policy towards Maldives. These self-interests have given rise to peculiar perception issues in the recipient country Maldives towards the Indian aid as discussed above.

Discussion

I have elucidated the development cooperation of India with Bhutan and Maldives in the preceding sections. Before

I analyse the issue further, it is important to understand how the China factor plays in India's aid equations with these two nations. I have described how the two countries, once in India's close embrace, have been willingly drifting towards China. China has undertaken a multidimensional strategy to increase its diplomatic and economic influence in India's neighbourhood. This strategy includes softer steps like scholarships and tourism, and more aggressive economic and strategic steps like the Belt and Road Initiative (BRI), bringing in massive investments in these countries and cementing the string of pearls policy of Chinese domination by gaining strategic bases in Indian Ocean around these countries (Ramachandran, Hariharan, & Mehta, 2018). Thus, China remains a common denominator in India's development cooperation policy for both Bhutan and Maldives. It is the increasing Chinese influence which has forced India to step up its aid quantum in Bhutan and Maldives to emerge as the world's largest aid provider to both. This clearly reflects on the 'needy donor' status of India underlining the need to provide such aid. India clearly understands that if it retracts in its development cooperation with Bhutan and Maldives, China is eagerly waiting to fill in with even bigger largesse.

The China factor is the reason India's aid motives seem similar in both countries – geostrategic and economic. The internal security motive is also common in both cases. Energy security is a motive which is peculiar to Bhutan due to its hydropower potential whereas religious fundamentalism is a critical concern for India in Maldives. Indian aid motives, carefully planned and executed, have been evolving with time in both the cases, in tune with the dynamic geo-political scenario. This has been evident in how India has been wary of involving itself with the Maldivian opposition lately. But, as I have discussed already, the development cooperation between India-Bhutan and India-Maldives is skewed in favour of India, in so far as the economic and commercial benefits accruing from such cooperation are concerned. So, in this respect, Indian aid, though mutually beneficial as a policy, benefits India more. Similar has been the experience in case of Indian development cooperation being untied and unconditional. Majority of Indian aid to both countries being project-specific, is bound by conditions in Lines of Credit (LOCs) agreements, and executed by Indian companies or companies with Indian partners. But it is also not totally tied, as the project choice has been the prerogative of aid recipient countries – Bhutan and Maldives.

This nature of Indian aid has given rise to negative popular and political perception of India's development cooperation in both countries. China has greatly benefitted from this and has been quite successful in making economic and diplomatic inroads into both the countries. Though Bhutan has still been wary of Chinese efforts to increase its influence, Maldives has openly accepted China as its ally in development. It is paradoxical that India as a donor 'needs' to provide ever-increasing aid to Bhutan and Maldives as the largest donor for both, and yet is perceived negatively. There is a need to comprehensively analyse this anomaly and take corrective action on the part of India. Any Indian response to a domestic situation in these two nations, should be diplomatic as a preferred choice before resorting to any other method such as the instances of direct involvement. Because any perceived adverse response, seen as 'interference', has the potential to turn into long-term strategic divergence, leading to fissures in the bilateral relations, prone to be filled in promptly by third parties like China.

As a policy, India choosing to leverage its economic assistance in the form of development cooperation to Bhutan and Maldives, to influence the political atmosphere in these countries furthering its own interests, has not been without its problems. In fact, India has allowed itself to be seen as interfering, leading to a recipient perception that India's model of aid is not truly mutually gainful (Stobdan, 2017) and this perception is not merely popular, but political too (Manoharan, 2014). Therefore, there is a need to have a policy tweaking of India's aid program so that it can be seen as truly mutually beneficial and non-interfering.

Conclusion

In this chapter, I have analysed whether and how India's aid policy as a donor is guided by its self-interest motives. I have begun by tracing the historical background of India's foreign aid program, its evolution over time and the policy shifts in this program to deal with the immediate neighbourhood and extended neighbourhood of India as a tool of India's foreign policy. Then, I have identified the key theoretical concepts like Global South, South-South Cooperation and its difference from traditional Northern Aid, donor motives, India's development assistance in South-South Cooperation, India as a needy donor, India's national interests and aid motives, and India's aid canvass. I have explained each of these to set the concept and context of my objective. After this, I have justified the selection of India's two aid partners – Bhutan and Maldives and explained how these cases lead to distinctive contextual findings. Further, I have elaborated these two cases in terms of India's aid spectrum including the major areas of development cooperation between India and these countries, significance of these two in terms of India's donor motives for them, mutually beneficial development cooperation and recipient perception for Indian aid in these recipient countries, with a brief sum-up of each case in terms of India's self-interests underlying the Indian aid. Then, I have highlighted the significance of the China factor in India's aid equation with these two recipients and analysed how and why India's aid motives for Bhutan and Maldives are influenced and shaped by Chinese attempts to gain diplomatic and economic inroads into both countries. I have also identified the motives of Indian aid which are similar, as well as which are different for these two recipients and the reason for such similarities and differences. Based on this discussion, I have supported my statement that India's aid motives as a donor for Bhutan and Maldives have been evolving over time and have been carefully planned, rather than being ad-hoc, in tune with the dynamic geo-political scenario in India's neighbourhood. I have also acknowledged that though Indian aid is mutually beneficial, yet the aid benefits are skewed in favour of India. This aid is untied and unconditional, but it is bound by the terms and conditions of aid instruments like the Lines of Credit (LOCs) or grants, though the choice of project has remained the prerogative of these recipient countries. I have also addressed the issue of negative popular and political perception of Indian aid in Bhutan and Maldives and the factors aggravating it, and how China stands to gain from this.

Bhutan and Maldives may be very small in size geographically and economically as compared to India, but both are vital to India's long-term stability, security and economic development. India as a donor has a much larger economic and geo-strategic stake involved in both countries. In both the cases, off and on, India has been involving itself in internal political crises and processes. China, taking advantage of this, is slowly emerging as a non-interfering ally, leading gradually to loosening of India's aid-led hold over both. It is high time India starts leveraging its socio-economic and cultural links to create more and more goodwill delivered by its effective aid program. It is in India's interests to maintain a close bilateral relationship with both Bhutan and Maldives, as a buffer against China, to counter aggressive Chinese strategy to ringfence India in its own neighbourhood. Bhutan and Maldives have the potential to emerge as the best bets for India in its neighbourhood policy and development cooperation program under the South-South Cooperation, provided India takes due care of these neighbours in terms of their aspirations and expectations from Indian aid. With fast changing geo-political climate not only in India's neighbourhood, but world over, India can indeed steer the evolving canvas of South-South Cooperation due to its long standing as a Southern donor and its commitment to mutually beneficial aid relations.

There are important policy implications of this study for India's aid program. India's foreign aid policy has always been guided by its self-interests, and has not become strategic all of a sudden. Whereas the self-interests like greater recognition in multilateral bodies, influence in immediate and extended neighbourhood, and projection not only as a soft power but also a hard power have been shaping India's aid policy, the recent motives to emerge as a world power and to promote particular strategic interests have given a policy shift to this aid policy. India still being a developing economy cannot leverage economic hard power to gain strategic goals in a similar way as China can do with its massive aid quantum. So, there is a need to judiciously practice a mix of both hard and soft power to expand India's aid sphere substantially to achieve the desired self-interests of India as a donor. Also, there is a need to expand the research horizon of this study to compare and analyse India's donor motives for the other development partners in similar geo-strategic settings like Nepal and Sri Lanka and also in different geo-strategic settings like the African nations, to understand whether the aid to these other recipient countries serves to achieve economic and political self-interests of India as a donor. The experience of Bhutan and Maldives has shown that Indian aid pattern has been evolving in line with the political will of the government of the day and recipient demands. Though this aid may be tied to Indian terms and conditions, yet it is not prescriptive. Though India's present aid policy, based on development cooperation, is based on the concept of mutual interests and benefits, yet it is guided by India's self-interests. To what extent does this Indian aid contribute to the development goals of recipient countries and their self-interests is a pertinent issue here, which needs further research and analysis of this aid policy from the recipients' point of view.

CONCLUSION

India has been experiencing consistently high growth rate over last 3 decades, coupled with gradual but steady gains in human development indices. Though the equitable distribution of these gains still remains a challenge, yet India's resilience during the global economic crisis of 2008 was widely acknowledged. Since 2011, UNDP has been including the country-wise IHDI – Inequality-adjusted Human Development Index, in its Human Development Report, which is distribution-sensitive average of human development level for that country. IHDI takes into account a country's progress in health, education and income and distribution of such progress among population in terms of equality. Theoretically speaking, IHDI and HDI become equal when perfect equality is there in generation and distribution of progress. Under distributional inequality, IHDI lags behind HDI, and more the lag, more the inequality. In the Human Development Report 2020, India's HDI was 0.645, whereas its IHDI was 0.475, meaning thereby that India's HDI lost 26% of its value when adjusted for inequality. This is an extremely critical element for development policy initiatives and also explains why successive governments have included faster, inclusive and sustainable growth targets in national development agenda. Reducing social and geographical inequalities of growth remains the guiding principle of national development policies.

India is home to 1.38 billion people as per 2020 estimates, and India's growth and progress affects the performance of development indicators globally. Over the years, India has shown that, with careful planning and focused intervention, development action works. India is making steady march forward to achieve the 2030 Agenda for Sustainable Development. One of the recent cases to demonstrate this is the way India has handled the ongoing Covid pandemic and earned international recognition for creating large-scale health infrastructure in its quest to provide health equity to all its citizens in terms of Covid testing, tracking, tracing, isolating and treating strategy. On economic front too, India has made remarkable strides. In 2015, India was the most preferred foreign investment destination in the world, ahead of the US and China, netting over USD 31 billion in foreign capital inflows. India's service sector, second only to China in terms of growth rate, has been growing in double digits in last few years.

India has adopted some of the most far-reaching and ambitious legislations in the world in its quest to reduce poverty and inequality. MGNREGA, Right to Education (RTE), Right to Information (RTI), Right to Food (National Food Security Act) are some of such progressive rights-based legislations, directly impacting poverty and inequality. Coupled with financial inclusion schemes like the Pradhan Mantri Jan-Dhan Yojana and skill development initiatives under the National Skill Development Mission, such interventions have emerged as the cornerstones of poverty reduction strategies in India, impacting the multi-level poverty. Programs such as the National Rural Health Mission (NRHM) and the National Urban Health Mission (NUHM) have gone a long way in providing health equity to the citizens. Other programs worth mentioning here are Housing for All by 2022 Mission, Clean India Mission and universal electrification under the Pradhan Mantri Sahaj Bijli Har-

Ghar Yojana (SAUBHAGYA), which strive to boost IHDI by emphasising on development and distributional equity.

Being world's largest and fastest growing democracy, India has emerged as a leader not only in South-South Cooperation, but also in key global and regional initiatives like BRICS, IBSA and SAARC. India has been at the forefront in sharing its development experience, knowledge and expertise with other developing countries around the world, without any prescriptive or extractive conditions. India's development cooperation has been promoting regional integration through trade relations, investment in infrastructure, training and technical assistance. India's growth over last few decades has been steady, stable, resilient and diversified; and without any prolonged or permanent reversals. This gives India a unique advantage as compared to other leading emerging economies of the world. This diversification is reflected in broad range of India's trading partners, trading basket and production structure which is not limited to a few products, commodities, services or natural resources; enabling India to absorb international slowdowns to a large extent without any substantial impact on its economy. This is also true of domestic major economic policy events such as the Goods and Services Tax (GST). When the GST was launched in 2016, there was widespread speculation that Indian economy would witness tumultuousness. But, barring a brief period between Q3 of 2016–17 and Q2 of 2017–18, when economy grew at below 7%, the growth remained stable. This is often seen as an aberration attributed to adjustments in domestic economic activities.

India has made great progress in its development journey since becoming independent in 1947, but it has had and still has its own share of challenges. These challenges are both external – a competitive international environment with pressure to integrate more and more with global economy; and domestic – issue of equitability with pressure to achieve better human development indices with inclusion and sustainability. India's development experience so far has infrastructure development and economic growth complementing each other, trying to get human development along in the process. In this scenario, it is imperative that India sustains a growth rate of 8% or higher, as economic growth is a pre-requisite for development. This means that the concerted reform efforts, which have so far remained the main-stay of India's development journey, would need to be sustained to maintain the growth momentum, with an emphasis both on human and humane development.

With an economy that has performed regularly at about 7% and has close to USD 500 billion of forex reserves, India has few lessons to offer for other countries too. One of the most pertinent of such lessons is about the possible outside intervention in the development process of another country. Further, India has to offer is on how development is hinged on improving and strengthening the state capacity in a democratic context. As the largest democracy in the world, India offers a rich experience to contribute to solving diverse global development problems. In the process, India needs to build upon the lessons learnt from its development experience so far. The insights into and introspection of India's development saga reflect the spirit and the dynamics of developing India, where the governance and policy must draw from the founding principles of equity and equitability enshrined in the Constitution of India, historical learnings from our civilisational history and present socio-cultural-economic context. A developed India would fulfil the aspirations of 1.38 billion Indians with a proud presence on the world stage.

To sum up, the way forward for India stems from its demographic dividend, which should be fruitfully leveraged through education, skill development, employment, technology and knowledge economy free from gender and socio-cultural biases. The sustained and ever-increasing integration with global political and economic situation has to be factored in at the level of policy formulation as well as policy implementation. The drivers of India's growth engine to catapult it into the league of developed nations are going to be pro-people development agenda, pro-active governance, participative and inclusive policies, sustainable development, and transparent and responsive government. A synergistic governance which evolves from a continuous partnership between public sector, private sector and civil society is the key to improve service delivery through participatory processes at all levels. Due to sheer size and diversity, no single model of development can be prescribed for transplantation into India, India needs to nurture its own growth strategy for achieving development.

BIBLIOGRAPHY

13th Finance Commission. (2009). *Report of the Task Force on Goods and Services Tax*. New Delhi: 13th Finance Commission.

———. (2015). *Explanatory Notes for State Formats*. New Delhi. Available at fincomindia.nic.in/writereaddata/html_en_files/oldcommission_html/fincom13

Abraham, G., & Samuel, J. (2016). *Future of Development Cooperation: Policy Priorities for an Emerging India*. New Delhi: Oxfam India. Available at www.oxfamindia.org/sites/default/files/WP-Future-of-Development-Cooperation-Policy-Priorities-for-an-Emerging-India-12072016.pdf

AFD. (2005). *Pro-Poor Growth in the 1990s. Lessons and Insights from 14 Countries*. Washington, DC: AFD (French Development Agency).

Agrawal, S. (2007). *Emerging Donors in International Development Assistance: The India Case*. India Focus: Partnership and Business Development Division (PBDD).

Agrawal, S., Basu, D., Ghosh P., Pareek B., & Zhang, J. (2019). *Tax-Pass-Through, Pricing Strategy and Consumer Spending Dyanamics: The Indian GST Experience*. SSRN. Available at ssrn.com/abstract=3396907

Alba, P., Hernandez, L., & Klingebiel, D. (1999). *Financial Liberalization and the Capital Account: Thailand 1988–97* (Policy Research Working Paper 2188). Washington, DC: Economic Policy Division, The World Bank.

Amnesty International. (2015). *Shifting Power and Human Rights Diplomacy: India*. The Netherlands: Amnesty International.

Aneja, U. (2019). South–South Cooperation and Competition: A Critical History of the Principles and their Practice. In E. Fiddian-Qasmiyeh, and P. Daley (Eds), *Routledge Handbook of South–South Relations*. London: Routledge.

Ashley, C. (2009). *Harnessing Core Business for Development Impact* (Background Note). London: Overseas Development Institute.

Asmus, G., Fuchs, A., & Müller, A. (2017). *BRICS and Foreign Aid* (Working Paper 43). AidData—A Research Lab at William and Mary.

Ayres, A. (2017). *Will India Start Acting Like a Global Power?* Foreign Affairs. Council on Foreign Relations. Available at www.foreignaffairs.com/articles/india/2017-10-16/will-india-start-acting-global-power

Bahl, R., & Martinez-Vazquez, J. (2006). *Sequencing Fiscal Decentralization* (Working Paper 3914). Washington, DC: The World Bank Policy Research Division.

Banerjee, K. (2010). *Social Development Report 2010*. New Delhi: Oxford University Press.

Bardhan, P. K. (1970). On the Minimum Level of Living and the Rural Poor. *Indian Economic Review, 5*(1), 129–36.

Basu, K. (2008). The Enigma of India's Arrival: A Review of Arvind Virmani's Propelling India: From Socialist Stagnation to Global Power. *Journal of Economic Literature, 46*(2), 396–406.

Basu, N. (2020, March 6). Oil, Chabahar, 'Violence Against Muslims': Why India-Iran Ties are Going into Free Fall. *The Print*.

Basu, S. (2009). Government Success, Failure of the Market: A Case Study of Rural India. *International Review of Applied Economics, 23*(4), 485–501.

Baulch , R., & McCulloch, N. (2000). *Tracking Pro-poor Growth* (ID 21 Insights No. 31). IDS, Sussex.

Bazoobandi, S. (2019). Mounting Sanctions Squeeze Iranian Exports. London: *Petroleum Economist*. Available at https://www.petroleum-economist.com/

Beck, T., Demirguc-Kunt, A., & Levine, R. (2004). *Finance, Inequality and Poverty: Cross Country Evidence* (NBER Working Paper 10979).

Bhadrakumar, M. K. (2020). Iran Loathes Pompeo's Chabahar Gift. Petrolia, California CA: *CounterPunch*. Available at counterpunch.org

Bhatia, R. (2018). *Maldives' New Balance*. New Delhi: Gateway House: Indian Council on Global Relations. Available at gatewayhouse.in/maldives-new-balance/

Bhogal, P. (2016). *India's Foreign Aid to South Asia*. Available at orfonline.org

Bhutan News Network. (2015). *Bhutan Elections: A Case of India's Diplomatic Bankruptcy!* Thimphu, Bhutan: Bhutan News Network. Available at http://www.bhutannewsnetwork.com/2013/07/bhutan-elections-a-case-of-indias-diplomatic-bankruptcy/

Bird, R. M. (2012). Subnational Taxation in Developing Countries: A Review of the Literature. *Journal of International Commerce, Economics and Policy, 2*(01), 139–61.

Bowman, E. H., & Hurry, D. (1993). Strategy Through the Option Lens: An Integrated View of Resource Investments and the Incremental Choice Process. *Academy of Management Review, 18*(4), 760–82.

Buchanan, J. M. (1966). *The Demand and Supply of Public Goods*. Chicago: Rand McNally.

Buchanan, J. M., & Vanberg, V. J. (1988). Politicization of Market Failure. *Public Choice, 57*(2), 101–113.

Calvo, S., Leiderman, L., & Reinhart, C. (1996). Inflows of Capital to Developing Countries in the 1990s. *Journal of Economic Perspectives, 10*(2), 123–39.

Carroll, T. (2012). Working On, Through and Around the State: The Deep Marketisation of Development in the Asia-Pacific. *Journal of Contemporary Asia, 42*(3), 378–404.

Center for Strategic and International Studies (CSIS). (2018). *India–Iran Cooperation at Chabahar Port: Choppy Waters*. CSIS Brief. Washington, DC: CSIS. Available at www.csis.org

Central Board of Indirect Taxes and Customs. (2019). *Goods and Services Tax (GST): Concept & Status*. New Delhi: CBIC, Ministry of Finance, Government of India.

Centre for Public Impact. (2019). *The Indian Government's E-Marketplace (GeM)*. New Delhi: Centre for Public Impact.

Chakraborty, L. (2019). *Indian Fiscal Federalism at the Crossroads: Some Reflections* (Working Paper No. 937). Annandale-on-Hudson, New York: Levy Economics Institute.

Chanana, D. (2009). India as an Emerging Donor. *Economic and Political Weekly, 44*(12), 11–14.

Chaturvedi, S. (2012a). India and Development Cooperation: Expressing Southern Solidarity. In S. Chaturvedi, T. Fues, & E. Sidiropoulos (Eds), *Development Cooperation and Emerging Powers: New Partners or Old Patterns*, pp. 169–89. London: Zed Books.

———. (2012b). India's Development Partnership: Key Policy Shifts and Institutional Evolution. *Cambridge Review of International Affairs, 25*(4), 557–77.

———. (2016). *The Development Compact: A Theoretical Construct for South–South Cooperation* (RIS Discussion Paper 203*)*. New Delhi: RIS.

Chaturvedi, S., Chenoy, A. M., Chopra, D., Joshi, A., & Lagdhyan, K. S. (2014). *Indian Development Cooperation: The State of the Debate* (Evidence Report No. 95) Brighton UK: Institute of Development Studies (IDS).

Choudhury, A., & Nagda, A.(2019). How India Funds the World: Financial Assistance in the Immediate Neighbourhood. *Economic and Political Weekly, 54*(22), 1–12. Available at https://www.epw.in/engage/article/how-india-funds-world-financial-assistance

Coase, R. H. (1974). The Lighthouse in Economics. *The Journal of Law and Economics, 17*(2), 357–76.

Cornes, R., and T. Sandler. (1996). *The Theory of Externalities, Public Goods, and Club Goods*. Cambridge: Cambridge University Press.

CQ Almanac. (1967). *Food for India* (23rd Ed.). Washington, DC: CQ Press.

Crockett, A. (2000). How Should Financial Market Regulators Respond to the New Challenges of Global Economic Integration (Paper presented in conference on Global Economic Integration: Opportunities and Challenges, Jackson

Hole, Wyoming). *Conference Proceedings by Federal Reserve Bank of Kansas City.*

Dahl-Ostergaard, T. (2005). *Lessons Learned on the Use of Power and Drivers of Change Analyses in Development Cooperation.* GOVNET Review. OECD DAC Network on Governance.

Das, S. (2019). 'Some Thoughts on Fiscal Federalism', speech, at the Book Launch 'Indian Fiscal Federalism', Mumbai.

Datareportal. (2020). *Digital 2020: India.* Available at www.datareportal.com/reports/digital-2020-india

Datta-Chaudhuri, M. (1990). Market Failure and Government Failure. *Journal of Economic Perspectives, 4*(3), 25–39.

de Janury, A., & Sadoulet, E. (2000). Growth, Poverty, and Inequality in Latin America: A Causal Analysis, 1970-94. *Review of Income and Wealth, 46*(3), 267–87.

Deininger, K., & Yanyan, L. (2013). *Welfare and Poverty Impacts of India's National Rural Employment Guarantee: Evidence from Andhra Pradesh* (Policy Research Working Paper 6543). The World Bank, Washington, DC.

Demirguc-Kunt, A., & Detragiache, E.. (1998). *Financial Liberalisation and Financial Fragility* (Working Paper No. 1917). Washington, DC: The World Bank.

Department for International Development (DFID). (2004). *What is Pro-poor Growth and Why do We Need to Know?* (Pro-Poor Growth Briefing Note 1). Policy Division, DFID, London.

Desai, S., Vashishtha, P., & Joshi, O. (2015). *Mahatma Gandhi National Rural Employment Guarantee Act: A Catalyst for Rural Transformation.* National Council of Applied Economic Research, New Delhi, India.

Devulapally, I. (2018, February 25). Chabahar Challenge. *Telangana Today*. Available at www.telanganatoday.com

Diamond, D. W., & Dybvig, P. H. (1983). Bank Runs, Deposit Insurance, and Liquidity. *Journal of Political Economy, 91*(3), 401–19.

Dikshit, S. (2016, July 16). India's Withdrawal of Cooking Gas Subsidy and Bhutan Politics. *The Hindu*. Available at http://www.thehindu.com/todays-paper/indias-withdrawal-of-cooking-gas-subsidy-and-bhutan-politics/article4919218.ece

Dollar, D., & Kraay, A. (2000). *Growth is Good for the Poor.* The World Bank.

Drabu, H. (2019). *Comments on Indian Fiscal Federalism: Any Link between GST Council and Finance Commission*, Panel on 'Indian Fiscal Federalism', the India International Centre. New Delhi.

Dreher, A. (2011). Are 'New' Donors Different? Comparing the Allocation of Bilateral Aid between Non-DAC and DAC Donor Countries. *World Development, 39*(11), 1950–1968.

Dreher, A., Fuchs, A., & Nunnenkamp, P. (2013). New Donors. *International Interactions, 39(3)*, 402–15.

Dutt, S. (1980). Indian Aid to Co-developing Countries. *Economic and Political Weekly, 15*(5), 672–78.

Dutta, P., Murgai, R., Ravallion, M., & van de Walle, D. (2014). *Right to Work? Assessing India's Employment Guarantee Scheme in Bihar.* Washington, DC: The World Bank.

Eastwood, R., & Lipton, M. (2000). Pro-poor Growth and Pro-poor Poverty Reduction: Meaning, Evidence, and Policy Implications. *Asian Development Review, 18*(2), 22–58.

Evenson, R. E., & Mohan, R. (1974). *The Intensive Agricultural Districts Program in India: A New Evaluation* (Centre Discussion Paper No. 198). Connecticut: Yale University.

Express News Service. (2019, December 14). India, Maldives Renew Joint Bid Against Terror. New Delhi: *The New Indian Express.* Available at https://www.newindianexpress.com/nation/2019/dec/14/india-maldives-renew-joint-bid-against-terror-2075827.html

France24. (2019). *Iran Looks to Remote Port to Beat US Sanctions.* Paris. Available at france24.com.

Fuchs, A., & Vadlamannati, K. C. (2013). *India - The Needy Donor.* Virginia VA: Aid Data.

———. (2013). The Needy Donor: An Empirical Analysis of India's Aid Motives. *World Development, 44*, 110–28.

Furton, G., & Martin, A. (2019). Beyond Market Failure and Government Failure. *Public Choice, 178*, 197–216.

Government of India. (2019). *GeM Handbook*, Available at https://assets bg.gem.gov.in/resources/pdf/GeM_handbook.pdf

GLA Economics. (2006). *The Rationale for Public Sector Intervention in the Economy.* London: Greater London Authority.

Goodman, J. C. (2015). *Answer to Krugman on Market Failure: Government Failure is Worst*. Available at www.forbes.com/sites/johngoodman/2015/02/24

Gourinchas, P. O., Valdes, R., & Landerretche, O. (2001). Lending Booms: Latin America and the World. *Economia, 1*(2), 47–99.

Governance for Development. (2018). *How Government e-Marketplace is Revolutionising Procurement in India*. New Delhi: Governance for Development.

Government of India. (1998). *Economic Survey.* New Delhi: Government of India Press.

———. (2003). Budget 2003–04. Speech of J. Singh, Minister of Finance, 22–23.

———. (2005). *The Mahatma Gandhi National Rural Employment Guatantee Act, 2005 (42 of 2005)*. New Delhi, India. Available at www.nrega.nic.in

———. (2017). *The GST Saga: A Story of Extraordinary National Ambition*. Retrieved from The GST Council, Ministry of Finance, Government of India. Available at gstcouncil.gov.in

———. (2019a). Available at www.gem.gov.in

———. (2019b). Available at www.msme.gov.in/know-about-msme

Greeley, M. (2019). Poverty: Ideas in Development. Ideas in Development. Classroom Lecture 6. Brighton: IDS, UK.

GST Council. (2020). Available at gstcouncil.gov.in

GSTIndia. (2020, April 10). GST: Is It Truly a Threat to Fiscal Federalism in India? *GST India - Goods and Services Tax in India*. Retrieved from gstindia.com

Gulrajani, N., & Calleja, R. (2019). *Understanding Donor Motivations: Developing the Principled Aid Index* (Working

Paper 548). Overseas Development Institute (ODI). Available at odi.org/principled-aid-index

Haque, T., & Verma, S. (1988). Regional and Class Disparities in the Flow of Agricultural Credit in India. *Indian Journal of Agricultural Economics, 43*(3), 356–63.

Harvey, R. S., & Gayer, T. (2008). *Public Finance* (8th Ed.). McGraw-Hill International Edition.

Hennart, J. F. (1993). Explaining the Swollen Middle: Why Most Transactions are a Mix of Market and Hierarchy. *Organisation Behaviour, 4*(4), 529–47.

Humphrey, J., & Messner, D. (2006). China and India as Emerging Global Governance Actors: Challenges for Developing and Developed Countries. *IDS Bulletin, 37*(1), 107–14.

Husseinbor, M. H. (2016). Chabahar and Gwadar Agreements and Rivalry among Competitors in Baluchistan Region. *Journal for Iranian Studies, 1*(1), 82–99.

IMF World Economic Outlook. (2019). Available at www.imf.org/external/pubs/ft/weo/2019/01/weodata

Institute of Economic Growth. (2018). *Rapid Assessment of Natural Resource Management Component Under MGNREGA and its Impact on Sustainable Livelihoods.* New Delhi, India: Institute of Economic Growth.

International Finance Corporation. (2012). *Micro, Small and Medium Enterprise Finance in India.* New Delhi: World Bank Group.

International Fund for Agricultural Development. (2019). *Republic of Liberia Country Strategic Opportunities Programme 2020–2024–COSOP.* Rome: IFAD.

Jalles d'Orey, M. A. (2020). *External Finance for Rural Development. Country Case Study: Liberia.* London: Overseas Development Institute (ODI).

Jamnejad, M., & Wood, M. (2009). The Principle of Non-intervention. *Leiden Journal of International Law, 22*(2), 345–81.

Jenkins, B., & Ishikawa, E. (2010). *Scaling up Inclusive Business: Advancing the Knowledge and Action Agenda.* Washington,

DC: International Finance Corporation and the CSR Initiative at the Harvard Kennedy School.

Jha, R. (2013). *Indirect Tax Reform and Fiscal Federalism in India* (ASARC Working Paper 2013/09). ASARC, Australian National University, Canberra, Australia.

Kakwani, N., & Pernia, E. M. (2000). What is Pro-poor Growth? *Asian Development Review, 18*(1), 1–17.

Kaminsky, G. L., & Reinhart, C. M. (1999). The Twin Crises: The Causes of Banking and Balance of Payments Problems. *American Economic Review, 89*(3), 473–500.

Karthikeya, R. (2010). *India's Iran Calculus*. Washington, DC: Foreign Policy. Available at foreignpolicy.com

Keech, W. R., Munger, M. C., & Simon, C. (2012). *Market Failure and Government Failure*. Presented at Public Choice World Congress. Miami, USA.

Kelkar, V. (2019). *Towards India's New Fiscal Federalism* (Working Paper No. 252). New Delhi: National Institute of Public Finance and Policy (NIPFP).

Keller, M. R., & Block, F. (2013). Explaining the Transformation in the US Innovation System: The Impact of a Small Government Program. *Socio-Economic Review, 11*(4), 629–56.

Kingsbury, D., Remenyi, J., Mckay, J., & Hunt, J. (2004). *Reassessing Development Theory: Modernization and Beyond*. Basingstoke: Palgrave Macmillan.

Klasen, S. (2005). *Economic Growth and Poverty Reduction: Measurement and Policy Issues* (Working Paper No. 246). Paris: OECD Development Centre.

Klonner, S., & Oldiges, C. (2014). *Safety Net for India's Poor or Waste of Public Funds? Poverty and Welfare in the Wake of the World's Largest Job Guarantee Program* (Working Paper, Discussion Paper Series, No. 564). Department of Economics, University of Heidelberg.

Kochar, A. (2008). The Effectiveness of India's Anti-Poverty Programmes. *The Journal of Development Studies, 44*(9), 1289–1308.

Kose, M. A., Prasad, E. S., & Terrones, M. E. (2005). *How Do Trade and Financial Integration Affect the Relationship Between Growth and Volatility?* (IMF Working Paper WP/05/19). Asia and Pacific Department and Research Department, International Monetary Fund.

Kraay, A. (2004). *When is Growth Pro-poor? Evidence from a Panel of Countries* (Policy Research Working Paper No. 3225). Washington, DC: The World Bank.

Kragelund, P. (2008). The Return of Non-DAC Donors to Africa: New Prospects for African Development? *Development Policy Review, 26*(5), 555–84.

Krugman, P. R. (1979). A Model of Balance-of-Payments Crises. *Journal of Money, Credit and Banking, 11*(3), 311–25.

Kumar, A. (2016). India–Maldives Relations: Is the Rough Patch Over? *Indian Foreign Affairs Journal, 11*(2), 153–67.

Kumar, Y. (2016). *India's Policy Towards its Extended Neighbourhood and the Larger Context of National Foreign Policy Challenges*. Distinguished Lectures. Gangtok, Sikkim: Ministry of External Affairs, Government of India.

Lafargue, F. (2006). L'Inde en Afrique: Logiques et Limites d'une Politique. *Afrique Contemporaine, 219*(3), 137–48.

Lal, S. (2018). *How Government e-Marketplace is Revolutionizing Procurement in India*. Available at blogs.worldbank.org: blogs.worldbank.org

Layard, R. (2005). *Happiness: Lessons from a New Science*. USA: The Penguin Press.

Leightner, J. E. (1999). Globalisation and Thailand's Financial Crisis. *Journal of Economic Issues, XXXIII*(2), 367–73.

Leightner, J. E., & Knox Lovell, C. A. (1998). The Impact of Financial Liberalisation on the Performance of Thai Banks. *Journal of Economics and Business, 50*(2), 115–31.

Levine, R. (2005). Finance and Growth: Theory and Evidence. In P. Aghion, and S. Durlauf (Eds), *Handbook of Economic Growth* (Vol. 1). Amsterdam: Elsevier.

Likoko, E., & Kini, J. (2017). Inclusive Business: A Business Approach to Development. *Current Opinion in Environmental Sustainability*, *24*, 84–88.

Lopez, J. H. (2004). *Pro-poor Growth: A Review of What We Know (and of What We Don't)*. The World Bank.

Makortoff, K. (2019, September 27). Thomas Cook Rescue Effort Brings Back Half of All Holidaymakers. *The Guardian*. Available at https://www.theguardian.com/business/2019/sep/27/thomas-cook-rescue-effort-brings-back-half-of-all-holidaymakers

Manoharan, N. (2014). *An Agenda for the New Government: Policy Options for India in Maldives* (Issue Brief 250). New Delhi: Institute of Peace and Conflict Studies (IPCS). Available at ipcs.org/issue_select.php?recNo=557

Marlow, I., & Dilawar, I. (2018). India's Grip on Strategic Port Loosens as Iran Turns to China. *The Economic Times*, 11 April. Available at economictimes.com

Mascagni, J. (2016). *Is Fiscal Decentralisation Delivering on its Promises? A Review of the Theory and Practice in Developing Countries* (IDS Working Paper 466). Brighton, UK: Institute of Development Studies (IDS).

Mawdsley, E. (2010). Non-DAC Donors and the Changing Landscape of Foreign Aid: The (in) Significance of India's Development Cooperation with Kenya. *Journal of Eastern African Studies*, *4*(2), 361–79.

———. (2012a). *From Recipients to Donors: Emerging Powers and the Changing Development Landscape*. London: Zed Books.

———. (2012b). The Changing Geographies of Foreign Aid and Development Cooperation: Contributions from Gift Theory. *Transactions of the Institute of British Geographers*, *37*(2), 256–72.

Mazzucato, M. (2013). *The Entrepreneurial State: Debunking the Public Vs. Private Myth in Risk and Innovation*. London: Anthem Press.

McCarthy, J., Canziani, O. F., Leary, N. A., Dokken, D. J., & White, K.S. (2001). *Climate Change 2001: Impacts, Adaptation, and Vulnerability.* Third Assessment Report of the Intergovernmental Panel on Climate Change. Cambridge: Cambridge University Press.

McCulloch, N., & Baulch, B. (1999). *Assessing the Poverty Bias of Economic Growth: Methodology and an Application to Andhra Pradesh and Uttar Pradesh* (Working Paper). Institute of Development Studies, UK.

McFalls, R. (2017). Inclusive Business: Profitable Business for Successful Development. In P. U. Petit (Ed.), *Earth Capitalism: Creating a New Civilisation through a Responsible Market Economy.* New York: Routledge.

McKay, A. (2005). *Tools for Analyzing Growth and Poverty: An Introduction.* Prepared as Part of the 'Operationalizing Pro-Poor Growth' Work Programme. DFID Pro-Poor Growth Team, Washington, DC.

McKinnon, R., & Pill, H. (1997). Credible Economic Liberalisation and Overborrowing. *American Economic Review, 87*(2), 189–93.

Mendelsohn, R. (2003). Assessing the Market Damages from Climate Change. In J. Griffin (Ed.), *Global Climate Change: The Science, Economics, and Politics*, pp. 92–113. UK: Edward Elgar Publishing.

Ministry of External Affairs. (2002). *Annual Report 2000–2001.* New Delhi: Ministry of External Affairs (MEA), Government of India. Available at meaindia.nic.in/annualreport

———. (2007). *Indo-Bhutan Friendship Treaty.* New Delhi, India: Ministry of External Affairs (MEA), Government of India. Available at www.mea.gov.in/Images/pdf/india-bhutan-treaty-07.pdf

———. (2014). *India–Maldives Relations.* New Delhi: Ministry of External Affairs (MEA), Government of India. Available at mea.gov.in/Portal//ForeignRelation/Maldives_December_2014.pdf

———. (2016). *Outcome Budget 2016–17.* New Delhi: Ministry of External Affairs (MEA), Government of India. Available at mea.gov.in/Uploads/PublicationDocs/26823_1-MEA_Outcome_2016-17_English_1.pdf

———. (2017). *India–Bhutan Relations*. New Delhi, India: Ministry of External Affairs (MEA), Government of India. Available at www.mea.gov.in/Portal/ForeignRelation/Bhutan-September-2017-en.pdf

———. (2018). *Annual Report 2015–16*. New Delhi: Ministry of External Affairs (MEA), Government of India. Available at www.mea.gov.in/Uploads/PublicationDocs/26525_26525_External_Affairs_English_AR_2015-16_Final_compressed.pdf

———. (2019). *India–Maldives Bilateral Relations*. New Delhi: Ministry of External Affairs (MEA), Government of India. Available at mea.gov.in/Portal/ForeignRelation/India_Maldives_Bilateral_Relations.pdf

Mishkin, F. (2003). Financial Policies and the Prevention of Financial Crises in Emerging Market Countries. In M. Feldstein (Ed.), *Economic and Financial Crises in Emerging Market Continues*. Chicago: University of Chicago Press.

Mohan, R. (2009). *Global Financial Crisis: Causes, Impact, Policy Responses and Lessons* (Working Paper No. 407). 1–38. Stanford Center for International Development, Stanford University.

Montreevat, S., & Rajan, R. S. (2001). *Financial Crisis, Bank Restructuring and Foreign Bank Entry: An Analytic Case Study of Thailand* (Discussion Paper No. 0131). Adelaide: Centre for International Economic Studies, Adelaide University.

Moser, T. (2003). What is International Financial Contagion? *International Finance*, *6*(2), 157–78.

Mukherjee, S. (2019). *Inter-Governmental Fiscal Transfers in the Presence of Revenue Uncertainity: The Case of Goods and Services Tax (GST) in India* (Working Paper No. 255), National Institute of Public Finance and Policy (NIPFP), New Delhi.

Mukherjee, S., & Rao, K. R. (2019). Impact of GST and What might Happen? In S. Mukherjee and K. R. Rao, *Evolution of Goods and Services Tax (GST) in India*, pp. 166–81. Cambridge, Massachussetts: Cambridge University Press.

Murrey, A. (2019). 'When Spider Webs Unite They Can Tie Up a Lion': Anti-racism, Decolonial Options and Theories from the South. In E. Fiddian-Qasmiyeh, and P. Daley (Eds), *Routledge Handbook of South–South Relations*. London: Routledge.

Mwase, N., & Yang, Y. (2012). *BRICs' Philosophies for Development Financing and their Implications for LICs* (IMF Working Paper, 12/74). Washington, DC: International Monetary Fund.

Ndlovu-Gatsheni, S. J., & Tafira, K. (2019). The Invention of the Global South and the Politics of South–South Solidarity. In E. Fiddian-Qasmiyeh, and P. Daley (Eds), *Routledge Handbook of South–South Relations*. London: Routledge.

Nelson, J., & Prescott, D. (2008). *Business and the Millennium Development Goals: A Framework for Action* (2nd Ed.). New York: UNDP-International Business Leaders Forum.

Nigam, S. (2015). The Challenges Faced Across South–South Cooperation. *Journal of World Economic Research, 4*(5–1), 27–32.

Obstfeld, M. (2009). International Finance and Growth in Developing Countries: What Have We Learned? *Frontiers of Research on Financial Globalisation, 56(1)*, 63111. IMF Staff Papers published by Palgrave MacMillan Journals on behalf of the IMF.

Organisation for Economic Co-operation and Development. (2001). *Poverty Reduction, The DAC Guidelines*, p. 39. Paris: OECD Publishing.

———. (2005). *Paris Declaration on Aid Effectiveness. Ownership, Harmonisation, Alignment, Results and Mutual Accountability*. Statement Endorsed at the High Level Forum on Aid Effectiveness. Paris: OECD.

———. (2007). *Promoting Pro-Poor Growth: Policy Guidelines for Donors*. Paris: OECD.

———. (2017). *Distribution of Net ODA (Indicator)*. Paris: OECD.

Pattanaik, S. S. (2019). India's Policy Responses to China's Investment and Aid to Nepal, Sri Lanka and Maldives: Challenges and Prospects. *Strategic Analysis, 43*(3), 240–59.

Pernia, E. M., & Quibria, M. G. (1999). Poverty in Developing Countries. In E. S. Mills, and P. C. Cheshire (Eds), *Handbook of Regional and Urban Economics* (Vol. 3). Amsterdam, The Netherlands: Elsevier.

Petru, M. R., & Alexandru, B. D. (2019). Government Failure vs. Market Failure: The Implications of Incomplete Information. *Theoretical and Applied Economics, XXVI, 2*(619), 91–104.

Plekhanov, A. (2007). Endogenous Corruption in a Federation. *The B. E. Journal of Economic Analysis and Policy, 7*(1), 1–29.

Prahalad, C. K. (2005). *The Fortune at the Bottom of the Pyramid.* Philadelphia, PA: Wharton School.

Prasad, E. S., Rajan, R. G., & Subramanian, A. (2007). Foreign Capital and Economic Growth/ Comments and Discussion. *Brookings Papers on Economic Activity, Issue 1*, Washington, DC.

PressTV. (2020, March 3). Investment Requests Pile up for Iran's Only Oceanic Port. *The PressTV*, Available at https://www.presstv.com/Detail/2020/03/03/620028/Iran-Chabahar-port-investment-India-US-sanctions

Prizzon, A., Chen, Y., & Jalles d'Orey, M. A. (2020). *External Finance in Rural Development: A Synthesis of Country Perspectives.* London: Overseas Development Institute (ODI).

Rajan, R., & Zingales, L. (1998). Financial Dependence and Growth. *American Economic Review, 88*(3), 559–86.

Ramachandran, S., Hariharan, H., & Mehta, S. (2018). *India–Bhutan Relations: Fostering the Friendship.* Takshashila Strategic Assessment. Takshashila Policy Advisory.

Ranade, A. (2019, September 20). Stronger Fiscal Federalism for Better Governance. *Deccan Herald.* Bengaluru. Available at https://www.deccanherald.com/opinion/main-article/stronger-fiscal-federalism-762881.html

Ravallion, M., & Chen, S. (2003). Measuring Pro-poor Growth. *Economics Letters 78*(1), 93–99.

Reddy, Y. V. (2019. New Approaches to Fiscal Federalism in India. *Review of Development and Change, 24*(2), 163–86.

Riddell, R. C. (2008). *Does Foreign Aid Really Work?* Oxford, UK: Oxford University Press.

Rivero, O. D. (2001). *The Myths of Development: The Non-Viable Economics of the 21st Century.* London: Zed Books.

Robson, P. (1984). *The Economics of International Integration.* London: Allen and Unwin.

Rodrik, D., & Subramanian, A. (2004). *From Hindu Growth to Productivity Surge: The Mystery of the Indian Growth Transition* (NBER Working Paper No. 10376). Cambridge, Massachussetts.

Rosenstein-Rodan, P. (1943). Problems of Industrialization of Eastern and South-Eastern Europe. *Economic Journal, 53*(210/211), 202–11.

Roy Chaudhury, D. (2017, February 6). Iran, India Trade Charges on Delay of Chabahar Port. *The Economic Times.* Available at https://economictimes.indiatimes.com

Rudra, A. (1971). Employment Patterns in Large Farms of Punjab. *Economic and Political Weekly, 6*(26), A89–A94.

Sachs, J., & Warner, A. (1995). *Natural Resource Abundance and Economic Growth* (NBER Working Paper No. W5398). Cambridge, Massachussetts.

Sarkar, P., Kumar, J., & Supriya. (2011). Impact of MGNREGA on Reducing Rural Poverty and Improving Socio-Economic Status of Rural Poor: A Study in Burdwan District of West Bengal. *Agricultural Economics Research Review, 24*, 437–48.

Sayer, J. (2006). Do More Good, Do Less Harm: Development and the Private Sector. In J. Sayer, and D. Eade (Eds), *Development and the Private Sector: Consuming Interests*, p. 18. Bloomfield, Connecticut CT, USA: Kumarian Press.

Schmukler, S. L. (2003). *Financial Globalisation: Gain and Pain for Developing Countries.* Development Research Group. Washington, DC: The World Bank.

Scott, D. (2009). India's 'Extended Neighborhood' Concept: Power Projection for a Rising Power. *India Review, 8*(2), 107–43.

Seers, D. (1969). *The Meaning of Development.* IDS Communication 44, Brighton: IDS.

Sen, A. (1987). *The Standard of Living*. Cambridge, Massachussetts: Cambridge University Press.

———. (2009). *The Idea of Justice*. Cambridge, MA: Belknap Press of Harvard University Press.

Shepsle, K., & Weingast, B. (1984). Political Solutions to Market Problems. *American Political Science Review, 78*(2), 417–34.

Singh, N. K. (2019). *Fiscal Federalism: Ideology and Practice*. 17th L. K. Jha Memorial Lecture. Mumbai: Reserve Bank of India.

Sinha, Y. (2004). *12th SAARC Summit and Beyond*. Seventh Dinesh Singh Memorial Lecture. New Delhi: Sapru House.

Smoke, P. (2013). *Why Theory and Practice are Different: The Gap Between Principles and Reality in Subnational Revenue Systems* (Working Paper 13). Andrew Young School of Policy Studies, International Center for Public Policy.

Son, Hyun Hwa. (2004). A Note on Pro-poor Growth. *Economics Letters, 82*(3), 307–14.

Srinivasan, S. (2015). *Assessing India's Infrastructure Aid Diplomacy*. New Delhi: Gateway House, Indian Council on Global Relations.

Srinivasan, T. N. (1979). Trends in Agriculture in India, 1949–50 to 1977–78. *Economic and Political Weekly, 14*(30/32), 1283–94.

Stiglitz, J. E. (2000). Capital Market Liberalisation, Economic Growth, and Instability. *World Development, 28*(6), 1075–86.

———. (2008). *Government Failure vs Market Failure: Principles of Regulation*. Presented at a Conference on Governments and Markets: Towards a New Theory of Regulation. Florida, USA.

Stobdan, P. (2017, July 14). India's Real Problem Lies in its Bhutan Policy, Not the Border. *The Wire*. Available at https://thewire.in/diplomacy/india-china-doklam-real-problem-bhutan

Stratfor. (2018). *Wary of China, India Shares its Largesse with Neighbors*. USA: Stratfor Worldview. Available at worldview.stratfor.com/article/india-china-aid-neighbors-nepal-bhutan-sri-lanka-maldives-bangladesh-seychelles

Stulz, R. M. (1999). Globalisation, Corporate Finance, and the Cost of Capital. *Journal of Applied Corporate Finance, 12*(3), 8–25.

———. (2005). The Limits of Financial Globalization. *Journal of Finance, 60*(4), 1595–1638.

Swaminathan, M. S. (1969). Scientific Implications of HYV Programme. *Economic and Political Weekly, 4*(1/2), 67–75.

Tanchum, M. (2014). Iran's Chabahar Port Transforms its Position. Tel Aviv: *The Jerusalem Post*. Available at https://www.jpost.com/opinion/op-ed-contributors/irans-chabahar-port-transforms-its-position-337167

Teodosio, A., & Comini, G. (2012). Inclusive Business and Poverty: Prospects in the Brazilian Context. *Revista de Administração, 47*(3), 410–21.

The Commonwealth Secretariat. (2020). *India: Constitution and Politics*. London: UK. Available at https://thecommonwealth.org

The Economic Times. (2019). *How an In-house e-Commerce Platform has Revolutionised Government Procurement*. New Delhi: Bennett, Coleman and Co.

The Guardian. (2001, March 15). *Annan Pleads with West as Environment is Pushed up UN Agenda.*

The Springfield Centre. (2015). *The Operational Guide for the Making Markets Work for the Poor (M4P) Approach* (2nd Ed.). The Springfield Centre. Available at www.beamexchange.org

The True Picture. (2019). *How is the Government e-Marketplace Driving Entrepreneurship and Transparency in India Today.* Available at www.thetruepicture.org

The World Bank. (1990). *World Development Report.* New York: Oxford University Press.

———. (2000). *World Development Report 2000/01: Attacking Poverty.* Washington, DC: The World Bank.

———. (2002). *A Private Sector Strategy.* Washington, DC: The World Bank.

———. (2005). *Economic Growth in the 1990s: Learning from a Decade of Reform.* Washington, DC: The World Bank.

———. (2006). *Global Development Finance: The Development Potential of Surging Capital Flow.* Washington, DC: The World Bank.

Tierney, M. J. (2014). Rising Powers and the Regime for Development Finance. *International Studies Review, 16*(3), 452–55.

Timmer, P. (1997). *How Well Do the Poor Connect to the Growth Process?* (CAER II Discussion Paper No. 17), Harvard Institute for International Development.

Todaro, M., & Smith, S. (2009). Classic Theories of Economic Growth and Development. In M. Todaro, and S. Smith, *Economic Development*, pp. 109–39. Boston: Pearson Education Limited.

Tolo News. (2019). *India's Work Over Chabahar Is 'Very Slow': Iranian Envoy, Kabul.* Available at https://tolonews.com/business/india%E2%80%99s-work-over-chabahar-%E2%80%98ver-slow%E2%80%99-iranian-envoy

Tytell, I., & Wei, S. J. (2004). *Does Financial Globalization Induce Better Macroeconomic Policies?* (IMF Working Paper 04/84). Washington, DC: International Monetary Fund.

United Nations Development Programme. (1994). *Human Development Report.* New York: Oxford University Press.

———. (1996). *Human Development Report 1996 – Economic Growth and Human Development.* New York: UNDP.

———. (2004). *Unleashing Entrepreneurship: Making Business Work for the Poor.* New York: UNDP.

———. (2008a). *Creating Value for All: Strategies for Doing Business with the Poor.* New York: UNDP.

———. (2008b). *Growing Inclusive Markets.* New York: UNDP. Available at growinginclusivemarkets.org

———. (2010a). *Rights-based Legal Guarantee as Development Policy: The Mahatma Gandhi National Rural Employment Guarantee Act* (Discussion Paper). New Delhi, India: UNDP.

———. (2010b). *Business Solutions to Poverty: How Inclusive Business Models Create Opportunities for All in Emerging*

Europe and Central Asia. Europe and CIS: UNDP Regional Bureau.

———. (2013). *Realising Africa's Wealth: Building Inclusive Businesses for Shared Prosperity.* New York: UNDP.

———. (2018). *South–South Cooperation.* Available at www.undp.org/content/ssc

———. (2020). *2019 Global Progress Report.* Paris: OECD and UNDP.

van der Meer, K., Noordam, M. (2004). *The Use of Grants to Address Market Failures: A Review of World Bank Rural Development Projects* (Agriculture and Rural Development Discussion Paper 27). Washington, DC: The World Bank.

Vossenberg, S. (2016). *Gender-aware Women's Entrepreneurship Development for Inclusive Development in Sub-Saharan Africa.* Gender Advisory and Knowledge Services. Amsterdam: Gender Resource Facility (GRF).

Weisbrod, B. A. (1978). *The Voluntary Nonprofit Sector: An Economic Analysis.* Washington, DC: Lexington Books.

Wescott, C. G. (2008). *World Bank Support for Public Financial Management: Conceptual Roots and Evidence of Impact* (Background Paper to Public Sector Reform: What Works and Why? An IEG Evaluation of World Bank Support). The Independent Evaluation Group (IEG), Washington, DC: The World Bank.

Williams, M. (2010). *Uncontrolled Risk: Lessons of Lehman Brothers and How Systemic Risk Can Still Bring Down the World Financial System.* New York: McGraw Hill Education.

Wolf, S. O. (2017). China–Pakistan Economic Corridor and Its Impact on Regionalisation in South Asia. In S. Bandyopadhyay, A. Torre, P. Casaca, and T. Dentinho (Eds), *Regional Cooperation in South Asia, Contemporary South Asian Studies.* New Delhi: Springer.

World Bank. (2002). *A Private Sector Strategy.* Washington DC: The World Bank.

———. (2005). *Economic Growth in the 1990s: Learning from a Decade of Reform.* Washington, DC: The World Bank.

World Bank Group. (2015). *India Development Update, April 2015: Towards a Higher Growth Path* (The World Bank Report No. 95979 – IN). Washington, DC: World Bank Publications.

Zeldes, S. P. (1989). Consumption and Liquidity Constraints: An Empirical Investigation. *Journal of Political Economy, 97*(2), 305–46.

Zerbe, R. O., & McCurdy, H. E. (1999). The Failure of Market Failure. *Journal of Policy Analysis and Management, 18*(4), 558–78.

INDEX

ABOUT THE AUTHOR

Vipin Sharma is an Indian Administrative Service (IAS) officer of 2005 batch, Maharashtra Cadre. His qualifications include MBBS, MA (Development Studies), Institute of Development Studies, Sussex, UK, MA (Public Policy) and PGDRM. He was awarded the prestigious Subhash Dua Memorial Gold Medal for the best performing Officer Trainee during IAS training at the Lal Bahadur Shastri National Academy of Administration, Mussoorie. His home state is Haryana; he is fluent in Marathi, Punjabi, Hindi and English.

He has vast experience in urban and civic administration, land revenue administration, rural development, development in Left-wing extremism affected areas, law and order administration, regulatory administration; and sectors including cooperatives and sugar, school education, and renewable energy. His administrative acumen and capabilities have been duly recognised both at the state and national level. He has represented India officially in the International Sugar Organisation (ISO) Plenary Sessions.

He has worked in various sensitive and challenging positions in Maharashtra. As Collector and District Magistrate Latur, his model of providing G2C (Govt to Citizens) services online through the Latur Setu Online became a role model in the State, with a provision of 354 G2C services in an online single-window system. As Commissioner, Sugar, he initiated the mechanism of calculating the sugarcane price by revenue sharing between farmers and sugar mills, which has been taken up by the Central Government for implementation in other sugar producing states. As Commissioner, Education, he looked after all aspects of school education in Maharashtra State from class 1 to class 12. This included around a million teachers, 23 million students and 1,08,000 schools, with a State plan budget of approximately Rs. 51,000 crore in 2017–2018 (~ USD 8 billion). As Director General, Maharashtra Energy Development Agency, he was responsible for achieving the renewable energy target of Maharashtra and last mile non-conventional electrification of rural Maharashtra. While working as the Additional Municipal Commissioner, Pune, he steered the effort, for which Pune city was ranked the most liveable city of India in City Liveability Rankings 2019–2020. Presently, he is working as the Civic Chief of Thane City, a bustling neighbourhood of Mumbai, where he has been successfully contributing to Covid management and mitigation since June 2020. He has been instrumental in Thane City being declared the best in Maharashtra in terms of environment conservation under Majhi Vasundhara Abhiyaan (My Earth Mission) in Majhi Vasundhara Rankings 2020–21.

Dr. Sharma has been a visiting faculty to the Yashwantrao Chavan Academy of Development Administration

(YASHADA), Pune and the Lal Bahadur Shastri National Academy of Administration (LBSNAA), Mussoorie, for the issues related to administration, governance, e-governance, development and public policy. He has participated in many programs related to development studies, leadership, change management, innovation and excellence in public service delivery, public finance, project appraisal, and participative democracy and inclusive development. An extensive traveller and avid reader, he is a staunch believer in democratic values and welfare state ethos, and strives hard to achieve them in his day-to-day functioning in the IAS.